Atkins Diet Plan 2021

The Ultimate Diet for to Lose Up To 30 Pounds In 30 Days and Feeling Great With 50+ Easy & Healthy Recipes

By

Lily Moore

Contents

Introduction

Given the reality that there are well over 1000 reported diets for weight reduction in lay literature, few have gained as much coverage as the Atkins Diet. This high-protein, low-carbohydrate weight-loss diet, which was published in his best-selling novel, The Atkins Diet Revolution, was created by the late Dr. Robert C. Atkins advocated the plan as an easy weight loss diet and a permanent improvement in nutrition. The diet has become increasingly common, enabling people to consume large amounts of meat and high-fat items without taking calorie limits into account.

The plan was pointed to by opponents as a high-protein, low-carbohydrate ketogenic, high-fat diet that might be harmful. Without scientific proof, early arguments from both sides were mostly filled by perception and personal perceptions. Eventually, the advent of several clinical studies demonstrated the effectiveness and protection of the Atkins Diet in the research literature. The Atkins diet is a low-carb diet, typically prescribed for weight reduction. A common low carbohydrate eating plan is the Atkins Diet. Although stressing protein and fats, the Atkins Diet excludes carbs (carbohydrates). Proponents of this plan say that, as long as one skip foods rich in calories, he or she will lose weight beside consuming as much fat and protein as one would like.

For weight reduction and maintenance, the Atkins Diet has many stages, beginning with a fairly low carbohydrate eating schedule. In several books, the Atkins Diet, officially named the Atkins Nutritional Method, has been presented in-depth and is credited with initiating the wave of low-carb diets.

About 20 research have demonstrated in the past 12 or so years that low-carb diets without any need for calorie counting are successful for weight reduction and may contribute to numerous health improvements. The diet, primarily because of its high saturated fat content, was initially deemed harmful and demonized by the conventional health authorities. New findings, however, indicate saturated fat is safe. The diet has also been extensively researched and proven to contribute to further weight reduction and better improvements than low-fat diets in blood sugar, 'healthy' HDL cholesterol, triglycerides, and other health markers. Although being rich in fat, on average, it may not increase "bad" LDL cholesterol, but this happens in a subset of people.

The key explanation that low-carb diets are so good for weight reduction is that a decrease in carbohydrates and improved protein consumption contribute to lowered appetite, without needing to worry about it, helping you eat fewer calories. Dr. Robert C. Atkins popularized a high-protein, low-carbohydrate, high-fat weight reduction diet that provides for limitless amounts of beef, eggs and cheese while severely reducing carbs, including candy, flour, noodles, milk, vegetables, and fruits.

Chapter 1: The Atkins Diet

The Atkins diet is based on the notion that insulin development is increased by consuming carbs, which contributes to appetite, eating, and weight gain. The hypothesis is that people experience diminished hunger on the Atkins diet and their bodies use processed fat for energy compared to burning glucose from consumed carbohydrates. It is claimed that consuming fat for energy results in weight loss.

1.1 Why should we choose Atkins diet?

One could opt to stick to the Atkins Diet because:

1. Enjoy the kinds and quantities of food included in the diet.
2. To help you lose weight, you want a diet that reduces those carbohydrates.
3. Want to modify the general eating patterns.
4. Had medical problems that you agree the diet will help change.
5. Like the related products from Atkins Diet, such as cookbooks, bars, and shakes.

If you are starting on Atkins, they will help you during the initial transition period, especially when you have been used to a high carb diet, where you might be craving sugar. Your cravings should fade after a few weeks on Atkins, but even then, low carb snacks will also play a major role by filling the stopgap in meals, so you do not get over hungry.

To help you lose weight and hold it off, the Atkins Diet is meant to modify your dietary patterns. Suppose you choose to reduce weight, maximize your stamina, or help strengthen some health conditions, along with high blood pressure and metabolic disease. In that case, the Atkins Diet often claims it is a safe lifelong approach to food.

Fewer carbs carry major benefits:

Atkins diet contributes to weight reduction but may also have a favorable knock-on impact on other aspects of your life. You get less bloated as you reduce the carbohydrates. Carbs help the body absorb water, so the clothes usually tend to fit better after a week or so.

A sudden increase in insulin levels accompanied by a crash that can make you feel weak, irritable, and exhausted is often triggered by high carb meals. You appear to have more stamina and fewer hunger cravings, and much more stable blood glucose levels. You may have found that the more candy you ingest, the more you like, but that sensation is gone, so it is a lot simpler to stick to Atkins.

Low carb meals filling:

As you consume foods high in dietary protein and fat that is usually more filling, you prefer not to feel hungry on Atkins anyway. The meals and treats you will eat are wonderful and not the typical boring meals that will make you fascinated with food. Plus, because you minimize the carbohydrates you consume, it is often simple to follow Atkins since you do not measure the grams or calories of proteins and fats.

Before beginning some weight-loss plan, consult with the primary care doctor professional since it will be even safer.

1.2 How does the Atkins diet works:

One of the well-known low-carb diets is the Atkins diet, and evidence suggests it can benefit. This diet could be the jump-start users need to lose weight if you load your day with refined carbohydrates such as white bread, noodles, and white potatoes and you do not consume enough fruits and vegetables.

When a human practice the Atkins Diet, their body's metabolism changes from consuming sugar, or glucose, as fuel to burning accumulated body fat. Ketosis is considered this switch.

Insulin levels are often down while glucose levels are low, and ketosis happens. In other terms, the body turns to utilize its fat reserves and saturated fats for energy while glucose levels are poor. This will, in turn, help a person lose excess weight and fat.

The glucose levels are low when human eats because their insulin levels have dropped as well. Their glucose levels increase while the individual consumes food, and the body generates more insulin into the bloodstream to help it utilize glucose.

You should avoid the normal go-to items and resume with the Atkins diet page. In food choices, the Atkins 20 plan's initial stage is minimal but based on low carb protein, vegetables, and fats that are not starchy. You add food groups to each stage: first nuts, seeds, berries, then fruits, starchy vegetables, whole grains, and beans. You will select from a greater range of foods and carbohydrates for the Atkins 40 package, but also with little or no starchy foods.

The closest you get to your weight loss target, the more range of foods you are allowed, with Atkins 20. Hopefully, you are trying to adhere to a balanced list and not go back to the old ways.

If you enjoy the wide variety of foods you consume, the Atkins 40 diet may be best for you. Of course, the portion sizes would also need to be held under check, which could be simpler since a low-carb diet can tend to tame appetite.

1.3 Is It good for certain Health conditions?

Shedding pounds will boost your health while you are overweight, and we know the Atkins diet succeeds. Although it is also unknown how long-term health is influenced by the greater amounts of animal fat and protein in the Atkins diet.

New evidence shows that those who preferred diets high in plant protein and fat on the Atkins diet did better for their health than others who went for the meat fat and protein-rich diet.

This concept is represented by the Atkins 20 and Atkins 40 diets. They rely mostly on consuming fats and protein from heart-healthy options such as olive oil and protein such as soy and lentils.

Before starting this plan, speak to the doctor, whether you have asthma, heart disease, renal disease, or elevated cholesterol, to guarantee that the balance of calories, fat, and protein is good for you.

1.4 Diet details:

For successful fat loss and health, the Atkins Diet's plan primary nutritional emphasis is eating the proper combination of carbs, protein, and fats. The Atkins diet allows one to lose weight by limiting sugar consumption, causing one to burn fat for energy instead of sugar. It often serves, in principle, to reduce cravings for those items. Obesity and associated health conditions like type 2 diabetes and cardiovascular failure are the faults of the traditional high-carbohydrate, low-fat American diet, as per the Atkins Diet. You do not need to skip fatty cuts of meat or cut off extra weight, as per the Atkins Diet. Instead of it controlling carbohydrates, is what is essential.

The Atkins Diet proposes that consuming too many carbohydrates contributes to blood glucose imbalances, excess weight and cardiac problems, particularly white flour, sugar, and other processed carbs. The Atkins Diet reduces sugars to the end and recommends consuming more protein and fat. The Atkins Diet states, though, that this is not a high-protein diet.

The Atkins Diet tends to change, like all diet programs. It now promotes more high-fiber vegetables to be consumed, accommodates vegan and vegetarian desires, and tackles health risks that might occur when a low-carb diet is begun.

Carbohydrates:

There is no portion control or calorie counting needed for the Atkins Diet. However, it does require you to watch your carbs. It utilizes a method named net carbs, which is the overall content of an item's carbohydrate minus its fiber content. For instance, there are 2.3 grams of total carbohydrate and 1.3 grams of fiber in a quarter (4 ounces) of raw broccoli, placing its total carbs value at 1 gram.

The Atkins Diet claims its carbohydrate solution would burn off the fat reserves in your body, monitor your blood sugar and help you maintain maximum fitness while not keep you feeling hungry or tired. The Atkins Diet also claims that it can help you determine your specific carbohydrate tolerance until you are at your target weight, the number of grams of net carbohydrates you should consume every day without adding or losing weight.

Exercise:

Exercise is not essential for weight reduction; the Atkins Diet says. It agrees, though, that exercising will help you control your weight and have other medical benefits.

1.5 Phases of the Atkins Diet:

The Atkins diet is separated into four distinct stages. If you have a BMI that is healthy? Then it is best to join Atkins' phase 3 or phase 4. The aim is to control your weight in these periods and become even more energetic. Are you obese, or do you want to easily drop weight? Atkins diet recommends beginning with phase 1 (where one can drop weight quickly) or phase 2. (in which one can lose more weight with time). The Atkins Diet's theory is that the body will drive to burn your fat reserves for energy if you count and limit carbohydrates, the natural fuel of the body, thereby encouraging weight loss. The key point is to avoid consuming processed flour and sugar, as with many other fad diets. But carb-dense whole-grain items are on the do not-eat list before one hit the maintenance level unless one attempts to obey the Atkins 20. There are four levels of The Atkins Diet. One may start with either of the initial three steps, depending on the weight loss goals.

Atkins Diet

PHASE I
Induction

PHASE II
Balancing

PHASE III
Pre-Maintenance

PHASE IV
Maintenance

1. **Phase 1: The Induction phase.** Under 20 grams a day of carbohydrate for two weeks. Eat high-protein, high-fat leafy greens such as low-carb carrots. This kick-start the reduction of weight. Users cut out with almost all carbohydrates from the diet in this strict process, consuming just 20 grams of net carbs a day, mostly from vegetables. They get just about 10 percent instead of having 45 to 65 percent of the daily energy from carbs, as prescribed for most diet recommendations. 'Base' vegetables should account for 12 to 15 grams of the daily net carbohydrates, such as asparagus, lettuce, cucumber, celery, green beans, and pepper. Users can consume protein such as fish and shellfish, seafood, beef, eggs, and cheese for every meal. Oils and fats do not need to be regulated, but one cannot include most vegetables, baked products, bread, noodles, wheat, nuts, or alcohol. One must drink eight glasses a day of water. Depending on the weight reduction, users can be in this process for at least two weeks. Because no grain-based foods are tolerated in Phase I, as long as you make sure you stick with gluten-free beverages and gluten-free salad dressing, gluten should not be a concern. The length of induction is up to two weeks.

2. **Phase 2: The Balancing phase:** Add more almonds, low-carb veggies, and limited quantities of fruit back to the diet steadily. In this process, as base vegetables, users continue to eat an average of 12 to 15 grams of carbs. one can probably need to avoid sugar-added items. One should steadily incorporate more veggies and fruit, nuts, and seeds to some nutrient-rich carbohydrates while people begin to lose weight. People continue this process once they are around 4.5 kilograms (10 pounds) from their target weight. One can consume anything they consumed in Phase 1, as in Atkins Phase 2, and incorporate fruit, cottage cheese (make sure you pick up a brand of gluten-free cottage cheese), almonds, seeds, and some juices. Again, no grain-based items are permitted, but one can comfortably eat gluten-free products in this step of the diet if none of the condiments contain gluten.

3. **Phase 3: The Pre-maintenance phase:** Add more calories to the diet while you are close to your target weight before weight reduction slows down. In this process, the variety of foods that one may consume, including starchy vegetables, fruits, and whole grains, will increase steadily. One should add approximately 10 grams of carbohydrates to their diet per week, so they must cut back once the weight reduction stops. If one hits the target weight, they remain in this process. Stage three of the Atkins diet is mainly gluten-free. Oats and brown rice are the only grains tolerated. But one could get into problems on the gluten front if one also reacts to oats or is just not particular

about selecting healthy oatmeal. Furthermore, certain people pursuing Atkins tend to fudge a bit by consuming a grain-based reward at this stage in the diet or getting a little sloppy, and this is when they can learn that they are susceptible to gluten (through unpleasant symptoms).

4. **Phase 4: The Lifetime maintenance phase:**

Here, one can eat as many nutritious carbohydrates without regaining excess weight as the stomach can bear. When you hit your target weight, you step through this process, and so you practice this form of eating for good. Some individuals chose to miss the induction stage and, from the beginning, have lots of vegetables and berries. This approach can also be quite effective.

Others tend to only remain forever in the induction process. It is also recognized as a ketogenic, very low-carb diet (keto). Step 4, meanwhile, is the maintenance phase of the diet, which provides for grain-based products, but the official diet plan recommends only wheat pasta, oatmeal, and brown rice. You should probably miss the wheat pasta to add only oatmeal and brown rice to maintain this gluten-free diet component but make sure to choose better quality gluten-free rice. **These stages, however, are a little complicated but are beneficial for the health. As long as people adhere to these phases and menu plans, they should shed weight and hold it off.**

Chapter 2: The Atkins Plan

A drop of carbohydrates is the pillar of the Atkins Plan. The diet has grown over the years to provide two choices at the moment. The initial step (Phase 1, Induction) for Atkins 20 is 20 g of' Net Carbs' (carbohydrate subtract grams of fiber) per day. The Atkins 40 makes 40 g of net carbohydrates a day at the starting stage. A rise in carbohydrates is allowed by both programs. One method introduces ingredients one at a time while the other improves the portion-size carbohydrate limit when persons reach their weight reduction targets.

The lifestyle, often referred to as the Atkins Dietary Approach, comes with three types today.

1. **Atkins 20 is for individuals who:**
   - Wants to shed over 40 pounds (lb.).
   - Have a waist diameter of more than 40 inches (men) or 35 inches (women).
   - Have pre-diabetes or diabetic type 2.
2. **Atkins 40 is for persons who:**
   - Wanting to drop less than 40 lb.
   - They are pregnant or nursing and choose to lose weight.
   - Need a diet for a broader range of foods.
3. **Atkins 100 is for individuals who:**
   - Want to keep their established weight.
   - They are pregnant.
   - Breastfeeding and attempting to hold their weight in check.

2.1 An Overview of the 3 Atkins Diet Plans:

Both forms of the Atkins diet rely on limiting what is considered net carbs (including those in vegetables) and stressing consuming protein and healthier fat types. Atkins describes net carbs as grams of carbs, excluding grams of fibers. When you start to approach your weight reduction target, pick carbohydrates, and introduce them into your diet. Atkins 20 and Atkins 40 involve different stages, while Atkins 100 is known to be a dietary plan and aims for no more than 100 net carbs per day to be eaten. Your initial 'induction' period in Atkins 20 restricts you to 20 grams (g) of net carbs, while your initial induction phase in Atkins 40 limits you to 40 g of net carbohydrates, offering you a little more versatility in the items that you can consume at the outset (including, for example, choosing fruits and some vegetables), You introduce net carbs back to the diet in 5 g increments (20, 25, 30, and so on) in Atkins 20, while in 10 g increments in Atkins 40, you add net carbs back to your diet, describes Lauren Popeck, RD, of Orlando Health, Florida.

The following chart details the diet guidelines for the first step of Atkins 20 (induction). Keep in mind that on Atkins 40, all these foods are deemed suitable (in small quantities).

a) Atkins 20 Food to eat:

You can eat any of the following foods to help jump-start your weight reduction on the Atkins 20:

- Veggies from the base, such as broccoli, lettuce, bok choy and cucumbers
- Protein, including poultry, eggs, and beef.
- Both seafood, including salmon, char, herring, and flounder.
- Butter and olive oil
- Few cheeses, namely cheddar, goat, Parmesan ham and swiss.
- Avoid: fruits such as pineapples and mangoes; starchy vegetables such as potatoes; and grains, initially at least.

b) Atkins 40 Food to eat:

It would be best if you consume any of the above plus the following foods while you are pursuing the Atkins 40 diet (as long as you hold net carbohydrates below 40 g a day).

- Nuts and seeds.
- Legumes (beans)
- Berries
- Starchy plants such as potatoes, carrots, and beets
- Whole grains such as rye, whole-grain rice, and spaghetti of whole wheat
- Avoid fruits such as mangoes and pineapples; starchy vegetables such as starchy grains and potatoes, initially at least.

c) Atkins 100 Food:

As long as you do not surpass 100 g of net carbohydrates a day, Atkins 100 supporters will consume nearly all foods. If you are consuming sugar or processed carbohydrates, carbs will add up easily, so it is better to restrict or stop them. There are no foods on the Atkins 100 that are deemed off limits. Even so, still on Atkins 100, you should expect to hold your carbohydrate consumption below 50 grams a day, but you may need to keep limited amounts of carbohydrate-rich items in order to sustain the target. Be sure you have in your diet a selection of various vegetables. There are four stages of the conventional Atkins diet, called Atkins 20. You should expect to cut down on your consumption of carbohydrates at each point, but the first, called induction, is the most restricting stage. In later levels, or whether you prefer Atkins 40 or Atkins 100, the consumption of carbohydrates would be better, but much smaller than the USDA's prescribed intake.

Chapter 3: What's In The Menu:

3.1 Preferable Foods:

- Foundational vegetables
- Shellfish and Fish
- Poultry
- Eggs, cream, and cheese
- Oils and fats
- Meat

3.2 Non-preferable Foods:

- Starchy vegetables
- Alcoholic beverages
- Most processed foods
- Seeds and nuts
- Sugary beverages
- Cereals
- Sweet treats and Junk foods
- Fruits and fruit juices
- Condiments, salad dressing and sauces
- Sweetened yogurt
- Grain and grain products
- Lentils and beans
- Crackers and chips

THE ATKINS LIFESTYLE FOOD GUIDE PYRAMID™

Whole grain foods such as
— barley, oats and brown rice

Vegetable and seed oils, cheese
and dairy, nuts and legumes

Fruits such as — blueberries,
raspberries, pears and avocados

Vegetables such as — salad
greens, broccoli, cauliflower,
asparagus and spinach

Protein sources such as
— poultry, fish, beef,
pork, and soy products

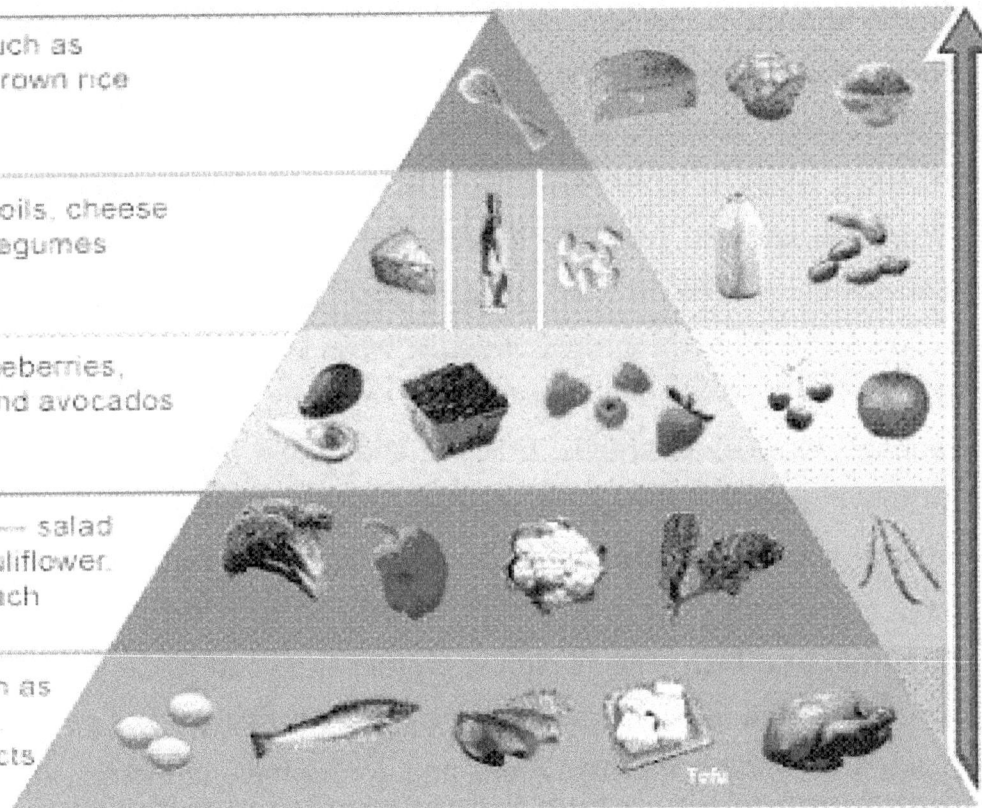

Tofu

INCREASE OPTIONS WITH ADDITIONAL EXERCISE

1. Preferable Foods:

An easy guide to Atkins 20, the Initial step is this "Acceptable Low Carb Foods List." By growing your
daily net carb consumption to an average of 20g a day, you can kick start induction during this process.

Among these, 12-15 grams must be in the form of foundational vegetables. Enjoy some of the meats, proteins, balanced fats, seeds and nuts, and most cheeses from collecting suitable low carb base vegetables below.

On these balanced ingredients, you can center your diet.

- **Seeds and nuts:** Walnuts, almonds, macadamia nuts, seeds of sunflower etc.

- **Foundational Vegetables**: Cauliflower, broccoli, cabbage, cucumber, brussels sprouts, kale, spinach, asparagus, bok choy, zucchini, olives, eggplant, mushrooms, cucumber, avocado, peppers, tomatoes, onions, lettuce, other leafy greens, etc. These are the lowest containing carbs in net carbohydrates and can be appreciated at all degrees of carb restriction. However, you will need to restrict your portions to certain kinds, such as bell peppers and Brussels sprouts, if you adopt a keto diet (< 20 grams of carbohydrates per day). In the Atkins diet, most carbs come from simple low-carb vegetables such as cabbage, lettuce, asparagus, broccoli, and others. It is important to know the number of carbohydrates in the vegetables that you consume. People at Atkins can aim and eat lettuce, cucumber, mushrooms, zucchini, broccoli, and 12-15 grams of net carbs each day.

- **Shellfish and Fish**: Fish is high in protein and good fats and is an outstanding source of vitamins D and B2, minerals and calcium such as iron and potassium. While all fish are Phase 1 acceptable low carb foods and do not have net carbs, Atkins suggest sticking to the styles mentioned here a few days a week for a 4-6 ounce serving., Because of the large levels of omega-3 fatty acids, fatty fish such as trout, salmon, sardines, mackerel, or herring are fine and may also provide health benefits. Everyone on Atkins is urged to eat a 4–6-ounce portion of seafood. Because of the calorie count, breaded fish is off-limits. However, some fish and shellfish, such as trout, tuna, halibut, cod, or flounder, are preferred. Appropriate foods contain shellfish such as shrimp, lobster, and clams. Oysters and mussels are all right at this point, but as they are higher in carbohydrates, it is recommended that you limit the intake to four ounces or less.

- **Poultry: Butter, cheese, milk, full-fat yogurt, full-fat dairy goods are preferable. Atkins recommends that between three meals, you divide the protein consumption and get it from various sources. Fowl is acceptable, like pigeon, turkey, duck, pheasant, and goose. 4–6 ounces are a recommended serving. Remember that cheese produces around 1 gram per ounce of carbohydrate, and Atkins suggests that you eat no more than 3-4 ounces of cheese a day. An ounce is around the size of a 1-inch cube or a slice of American cheese individually packed.**

- **Meat:**

A component of the Atkins diet may be beef, pork, lamb, eggs, bacon, and others. Acceptable meat forms include beef, pork, lamb, veal, and venison, and Atkins consumers are urged to serve meat in the correct serving size (4-6 ounces). You ought to be vigilant of some meat forms on the Atkins plan, including pork, sausage, and other cooked meats. These items can include added sugar since sugar is used to cure them. Atkins consumers are also advised to avoid meat containing nitrates and cold meat cuts.

- **Eggs, Cheese and Cream:**

Eggs on Atkins are a preferred protein source, e.g., The healthiest eggs are enriched or pastured with omega 3. There are certain carbs in cheese, but it is recommended for anyone on the plan to eat no more than 3 ounces a day. Any other dairy items may be eaten, such as cream and sour cream, but goat's milk, cottage cheese, yogurt and ricotta are not suggested.

- **Oils and fats:**

A significant aspect of Atkins is to consume a healthy quantity of fat. There are no sugars, but keep in mind that the maximum consumption indicated for added fats is 2-4 teaspoons a day. When cooking, do not encourage any oils to exceed extremely high temperatures and use olive oil to sauté. To dress cooked veggies or lettuce, use walnut or sesame oil, but not for frying. Coconut oil, extra virgin oil, avocados and avocado oil may be part of the diet Atkins. You can lose weight as long as you center your meals on a source of fatty protein with vegetables or nuts and other healthier fats. It is so simple. While there is a common belief that people consume large quantities of butter and other saturated fat on Atkins, this is not accurate. Followers of Atkins are recommended to retain 2-4 teaspoons a day of their added fat consumption. Mayonnaise, butter, olive oil, walnut or sesame oil are suitable fats.

- **Beverages:**

Since they are also a big source of secret sugars and carbohydrates, pay particular attention to your drinks. During Atkins 20, Phase 1, it is essential to consume at least 64 ounces of water a day. Drinking more fluid helps in weight control and is essential for maintaining health. Here are several beverages on the Atkins diet that are suitable.

1. **Water:** As always, the go-to beverage should be water. Keep making IT your drink of choice, as well as flavored or sparkling water, but be sure to read the list of ingredients to search for added sugars.
2. **Coffee**: Several tests indicate that coffee is strong and very high in antioxidants but is healthy. For weight reduction, black or with minimal quantities of milk or cream is optimal. Be sure to add loads of milk or cream, particularly if you often drink coffee during the day, even if you are not hungry. But feel free to use full-fat cream if you are starving. Or try coconut oil and butter called as "Bulletproof coffee".
3. **Green tea**: A very healthy beverage. In limited doses, alcohol is good as well. Stick to dry wines without added sugar and skip beer-like high-carb beverages.

In the Atkins plan, you must limit certain foods:

2. Non-Preferable Foods:

It is essential to select foods rich in nutrients but low in carbohydrates while adopting a low-carb Atkins diet. Few foods should be minimized, and others should be entirely avoided. In part, your decisions rely on your carbohydrate tolerance. Focus on consuming a selection of nutritious foods in the meantime.

- **Grains and Grain Products:**

A large variety of food items made from grains are used in the typical American diet. If you are in the initial step of Atkins 20, you must not eat certain items. Such products include bread, cereal, pasta muffins, bagels, and other baked goods. You are not going to eat carbohydrates like corn, wheat, or barley, too. Bread is a staple food in many countries. It appears in many types, such as loaves, bagels, wraps, and flatbreads, like tortillas. All of these are, however, high in carbohydrates. This is relevant for types of whole grain as well as those produced from processed wheat. While carbohydrate counts differ depending on the portion sizes and ingredients for common bread, here are all the average counts:

- ✓ **Whole-wheat bread (1 slice):** 17 grams of carbohydrates, 2 of them are fiber.
- ✓ **White bread (1 slice):** 14 grams of carbohydrates, 1 of them is fiber.
- ✓ **Bagel (3-inch):** 29 grams of carbohydrates, 1 of them is fiber.
- ✓ **Flour tortilla (10-inch):** 36 grams of carbohydrates, 2 of them are fiber.

Eating a toast, burrito, or bagel could bring you close to or over your daily limit, based on your carb tolerance. Make your low-carb loaves at home if you do want to enjoy the bread. Many grains are often rich in carbohydrates, like rice, wheat, and oats, and should be limited or eliminated on a low-carb diet like the Atkins diet.

Pasta is a staple that is versatile and cheap but very rich in carbohydrates. There are 43 grams of carbs in one cup (250 grams) of cooked pasta, about 3 of them are fiber. At 37 grams of carbohydrates, including 6 grams of fiber, the same quantity of whole-wheat pasta is just a marginally better choice. Eating spaghetti or other pasta forms is not a safe option on a low-carb diet because you eat a really limited amount, which for most people is not possible. Start making shirataki noodles or spiralized vegetables instead if you are wanting pasta but do not want to go off the carb limit. You will learn to use limited grains in your diet while you make progress on Atkins. You are encouraged to use whole grains, which are rich in fiber.

- **Cereal:**

It is well established that several carbohydrates are included in sugary breakfast cereals. You can be shocked, though, by the carb counts of balanced cereals. For example, 32 grams of carbs are provided in 1 cup (90 grams) of cooked, normal, or instant oatmeal, with only four fibers. Steel-cut oats are less refined and are generally considered better than other forms of oatmeal. However, 29 grams of carbs are present in a mere 1/2 cup (45 grams) of cooked steel-cut oats, including 5 grams of fiber. Whole-grain cereals are also more likely to pack even more. A 1/2 cup (61 grams) of granola comprises 37 grams of carbohydrate and 7 grams of fiber, whereas a massive 46 grams of carbohydrate and 5 grams of fiber is filled in the same quantity of grape nuts. A bowl of cereal might easily bring you over your total carb cap, based on your personal carb goal, before milk is added.

- **Fruit and Fruit Juice:**

Higher consumption of and vegetables and fruits has consistently been correlated with a reduced risk of heart failure and cancer. Many vegetables, though, are rich in carbohydrates, which may not be acceptable for low-carb diets, such as the Atkins diet. One small piece or 1 cup (120 grams) is a typical serving of fruit. For instance, a small apple produces 21 grams of carbohydrates, 4 of which come from fiber. It is probably a good idea to eliminate certain fruits on a very low-carb diet, particularly dried fruits, and sweet fruits, with a high carb count.

- ✓ **Mango sliced (1 cup / 165 grams):** 28 grams of carbohydrates, 3 of them are fiber.
- ✓ **Raisins (1 ounce / 28 grams):** 22 grams of carbohydrates, 1 of them is fiber.
- ✓ **Dates (2 large):** 36 grams of carbohydrates, 4 of them are fiber.
- ✓ **Banana (1 medium):** 27 grams of carbohydrates, 3 of them are fiber.

Berries are higher in fiber and lower in sugar than other fruits. Therefore, also on very-low-carb diets, small amounts can be enjoyed, about 1/2 cup (50 grams). In a low-carb diet, the juice is one of the worse drinks you might consume. While it contains certain nutrition, fruit juice is quite rich in fast-digesting carbohydrates, triggering a sudden rise in your blood sugar. E.g., apple juice containing 12 ounces (355 ml) holds 48 grams of carbs. This is also better than a drink holding 39 grams. For a 12-ounce (355-ml) serving, grape juice contains a whopping 60 grams of carbohydrates. While vegetable juice does not produce quite as many carbs as its fruit equivalents, there are still 16 grams of carbs in a 12-ounce (355-ml) serving, just 2 of which come from fiber.

What is more, the juice is another source of liquid carbs that might not be absorbed in the same manner as for solid carbs through your brain's appetite center. Later in the day, consuming juice will result in increased appetite and food consumption. Although there are many essential vitamins in fruit and fruit juice, these fruits and drinks often provide sugars and glucose, making them rich in carbohydrates. In the late stages of Atkins, you may add certain low-carb fruits to the diet; you should fully prevent them in the first phase of Atkins 20.

- **Starchy vegetables:**

Many diets allow an unrestricted consumption of vegetables that are low in starch. Most vegetables are very rich in fiber, which may promote weight loss and regulation of blood sugar. Some high-starch vegetables produce more digestible carb than fiber, but these vegetables on a low-carb diet should be restricted. What is more, if you are adopting a low-carb diet, skipping these starchy vegetables entirely is the safest choice:

- ✓ **Corn (1 cup / 175 grams):** 41 grams of carbohydrates, 5 of them are fiber.
- ✓ **Sweet potato/ 1 medium yam:** 24 grams of carbohydrates, 4 of them are fiber.
- ✓ **Potato (1 medium):** 37 grams of carbohydrates, 4 of them are fiber.

✓ **1 cup / 150 grams cooked beets:** 16 grams of carbohydrates, 4 of them are fiber.

Notably, on a low-carb diet, you can enjoy some low-carb vegetables.

- **Beans and Lentils:**

A good source of nutrients and protein is lentils, beans, chickpeas (for example, kidney beans, split peas, or garbanzo beans). However, since these items are often a good source of carbohydrates, most phases of Atkins 20 can inhibit them. Beans and legumes are healthy food. They may have several health advantages, including a lowered risk of inflammation and heart attack. While rich in fiber, they produce a decent quantity of carbs as well. You could be allowed to use minor quantities on a low-carb diet based on personal tolerance. Here are the carb counts for 1 cup (160–200 grams) of legumes and cooked beans:

  ✓ **Peas:** 25 grams of carbohydrates, 9 of them are fiber
  ✓ **Lentils:** 40 grams of carbohydrates, 16 of them are fiber
  ✓ **Pinto beans:** 45 grams of carbohydrates, 15 of them are fiber.
  ✓ **Black beans:** 41 grams of carbohydrates, 15 of them are fiber.
  ✓ **Chickpeas:** 45 grams of carbohydrates, 12 of them are fiber
  ✓ **Pinto beans:** 45 grams of carbohydrates, 15 of them are fiber.

- **Alcoholic Beverages:**

Alcohol on a low-carb diet can be enjoyed in moderation. Currently, dry wine contains very little carbohydrates, and hard liquor has zero. Alcohol is moderately heavy in carbohydrates, though. On average, a 12-ounce (356-ml) can of beer contains 13 grams of carbohydrates. There are also 6 grams of carbs in per can of light beer.

What is more, studies indicate that liquid carbs appear to facilitate weight gain more than solid food carbs. That is because liquid carbohydrates are not as filling as solid food, and the hunger does not appear to reduce almost as much. In the first step of Atkins 20, you will eliminate alcoholic drinks. You will start to appreciate these drinks in moderation and with caution from phase 2 onwards. Simple liquors seem to contain fewer sugars, but with sugar, mixers tend to be produced.

- **Sugary Beverages**

You are already well informed that things rich in sugar, including sweets, candy, and cookies, are off-limits on a low-carb diet. You do not realize that normal sugar contains as many carbs as white sugar. Currently, when weighed in tablespoons, many of them are even richer in carbohydrates.

Here are the carbohydrate counts for one tablespoon of various types of sugar:
  - ✓ **Maple syrup:** 13 grams of carbohydrates
  - ✓ **White sugar:** 12.6 grams of carbohydrates
  - ✓ **Agave nectar:** 16 grams of carbohydrates
  - ✓ **Honey:** 17 grams of carbohydrate

What is worse, little, or no nutritional benefit is given by these sweeteners. When carb consumption is minimal, selecting safe, high-fiber carb sources is particularly important. Choose a balanced sweetener instead of sweeteners of foods or drinks without consuming carbohydrates. Any flavored non-alcoholic drinks are made of sugar or chemical sweeteners. Sugary drinks are usually off-limits. Also, drinks produced with artificial sweeteners (sucralose, stevia, or saccharine) are tolerated. It is proposed that followers of Atkins restrict ingestion to the average of three packets a day.

- **Seeds and nuts:**

Another healthy source of fat and protein is nuts and beans, but they also raise carbohydrate consumption. In general, on the induction level of Atkins, they are not advised. However, you will swap three grams of net carbohydrates from vegetables for three grams of nuts or seeds if you have chosen to remain longer than two weeks in this phase.

- **Condiments, sauces, and Salad Dressing:**

On a low-carb diet, a large range of salads may be appreciated daily. Commercial dressings, however, always end up adding more carbs than you would think, particularly low-fat and fat-free types. Two tablespoons (30 ml) of fat-free French dressing, for example, includes 10 grams of carbohydrates. There are 11 grams of carbohydrates in an equal portion of fat-free ranch dressing. More than two tablespoons (30 ml), especially on a broad entrée salad, are widely used by several people. Dress the salad with a creamy, full-fat dressing to minimize the carbohydrates. It is better possible to utilize a splash of vinegar and olive oil, which can support weight control and is related to improved heart health. While several sauces and salad dressings are made from fat, added sugars are often used in most. Ketchup and barbecue sauce, for instance, are often rich in sugar. Salad dressings could also be a source of added sugar. Typically, these items are off-limits unless there is no natural or artificial sugar in them.

- **Sweetened yogurt:**

Yogurt is a versatile and nutritious food. While plain yogurt is comparatively low in carbohydrates, fruit-flavored, sweetened low-fat or non-fat yogurt is also consumed by several individuals. Yogurt that is sweetened also includes as many calories as a dessert. Up to 47 grams of carbohydrate can contain one cup (245 grams) of non-fat sweetened fruit yogurt, much greater than a comparable serving of ice cream. Choosing a 1/2 cup (123 grams) of regular Greek yogurt, though, topped with 1/2 cup (50 grams) of blackberries or raspberries, can keep under 10 grams of digestible carbohydrates.

- **Crackers and chips:**

The famous snack foods are chips and crackers, but their carbohydrates will easily add up. There are 18 grams of carbohydrates in one ounce (28 grams) of tortilla chips, about 1 of which is fiber. This probably 10-15 average-sized chips. Based on processing, crackers differ in carb quality. However, even whole-wheat crackers produce around 19 grams of carbohydrates per 1 ounce (28 grams), plus 3 grams of fiber. Processed snack items are usually eaten within a limited amount of time in significant amounts, so especially if you are on a carb-restricted diet, it is better to avoid them.

3.3 Food you may eat:

In the Atkins diet, there are many tasty items that you should consume. This involves things such as heavy cream, bacon, dark chocolate, and cheese. Because of the high-calorie content and high fat, most of them are commonly called fattening.

- ✓ **Unrefined grains:** Brown rice, quinoa, oats, and many others.
- ✓ **Tubers:** Sweet potatoes, potatoes, and some others.
- ✓ **Legumes:** Lentils, pinto beans, black beans etc. (if you can bear them).
- ✓ What is more if you want you can have the following in moderation:
- ✓ **Dark chocolate: choose organic products of at least 70% cocoa. Dark chocolate is rich in antioxidants, and if you consume it in moderation, it will have health benefits. However, if you eat too much, be careful that dark chocolate and drugs can inhibit your development.**
- ✓ **Wine: Select dry wines that do not contain artificial sugar or carbohydrates.**

Your liver, though, improves the usage of fat as an energy source while you are on a low-carb diet and suppresses your appetite, decreasing the chance of overeating and weight gain.

3.4 A typical day's menu on the Atkins Diet:

Here is a preview of what you might consume on a normal Atkins Diet day:

Atkins Diet Chart

9:00 AM
11:00 AM
1:00 PM
4:00 PM
8:00 PM

Total Fat 133 gm
Calcium 600 mg
Iron 17 mg
Sodium 1200 mg
Protein 125 gm
Carbohydrate 75 gm

TOTAL CALORIES
(kcals/Day)
2000

- **For breakfast.** Scrambled eggs sautéed with cheddar cheese and onions. Tea, coffee, water, herbal tea, and diet soda are suitable beverages.
- **Lunch.** Chef's salad with chicken, avocado dressing, and bacon, along with an acceptable beer.
- **Dinner.** Cherry tomatoes and cucumbers with baked salmon steak, arugula salad and asparagus, along with an allowable beer.
- **Snacks.** Usually, you can get two snacks a day.   An Atkins Diet product, such as a granola bar or chocolate shake, or a basic snack such as cheddar cheese and celery are acceptable.

3.5 A typical Week's menu on the Atkins diet:

Here's what a week of eating could look like on the Atkins 20 diet.

Day 1

- **Breakfast** Spinach and cheese omelet with salsa and avocado.
- **Lunch** Stir fried chicken roast.
- **Snack** mozzarella string cheese.
- **Dinner** Broccoli and chicken Alfredo with a salad.

Day 2

- **Breakfast** scrambled eggs with cheddar cheese and sautéed onions.
- **Lunch** taco bowl with beef, ½ avocado, tomato, onions, mixed greens, and green peppers
- **Snacks** Atkins Caramel chocolate nut roll Bar: Muffin made within a minute.
- **Dinner** fish with artichoke sauce, spinach, and cauliflower salad.

Day 3

- **Breakfast** Tomato, spinach, avocado and Monterey jack stacks.

- **Lunch** Atkins Frozen Orange Chicken.

- **Snacks** Atkins Milk Choco Delight Shake; 2 tablespoons (tbsp) cream cheese with 2 stalks celery.

- **Dinner** Stuffed Pork Chops with Fennel Gratinata, Fonduta and a broccoli.

Day 4

- **Breakfast** red bell pepper stuffed with spinach and eggs.
- **Lunch** Atkins Chocolate Peanut Butter Bar
- **Snacks** Atkins French Vanilla Shake; 1cup sliced cucumber with 2 tbsp of green goddess dressing
- **Dinner** Atkins Frozen Crustless Chicken Pot Pie; 1tbsp of olive oil and ½ cup of Brussels sprouts

Day 5

- **Breakfast** Atkins Frozen Cheese and Ham Omelet.
- **Lunch** Atkins Frozen Chili Con Carne with 2tbsp of Italian dressing and 2 cups of mixed greens.
- **Snacks** 2tbsp of ranch dressing with 1 cup of sliced red bell pepper and Atkins friendly Strawberry Shake.
- **Dinner** Cauliflower and Chicken Chorizo Sauté with sausage and cheese.

Day 6

- **Breakfast** Beef sautéed with onions and peppers topped with cheese.
- **Lunch** Atkins friendly Creamy Chocolate Shake
- **Snacks** Atkins friendly Caramel Chocolate Peanut Nougat Bar; 2 ounces of cheddar with 5 snap peas.
- **Dinner** Atkins friendly Frozen Beef Merlot.

Day 7

- **Breakfast** Atkins friendly Chocolate Almond Caramel Bar.
- **Lunch** Cobb salad.
- **Snacks** 2oz cheddar with 2 celery stalks; 2tbsp of ranch dressing with ½ cup of chopped red bell peppers.
- **Dinner** Portobello Mushroom Gravy with Atkins Frozen Meatloaf.

Here's what a week of eating could look like on the Atkins 40 diet.

Day 1

- **Breakfast** Spinach and cheese omelet with salsa and avocado and a slice of a bread of whole grain.
- **Lunch** Stir-fried roast chicken.
- **Snack** ¼ cup of blueberries or handful of walnuts.
- **Dinner** Broccoli and chicken Alfredo and a salad.

Day 2

- **Breakfast** Atkins friendly chicken chorizo cauliflower sauté with salsa and cheese.
- **Lunch** Chicken and kale Caesar salad.
- **Snacks** Atkins friendly Milk Chocolate Delight Shake with ½ small banana.
- **Dinner** ¼ cup of wild rice with 6oz of salmon, 2 tbsp of peanut butter with ½ cup of sliced cucumbers and 2 cups of mixed greens.

Day 3

- **Breakfast** Atkins friendly Vanilla Shake.
- **Lunch** Atkins friendly Frozen Shrimp Scampi with a small tomato, 2 tbsp of Caesar dressing, 2 cups of mixed greens and ½ avocado.
- **Snacks** 1 small carrot with ¼ cup of hummus; ½ cup of Greek yogurt with ½ cup of blackberries.
- **Dinner** Cauliflower Mash and Chimichurri Steak which are Atkins friendly.

Day 4

- **Breakfast** Oatmeal topped with ¼ cup of sliced strawberries and ¼ cup of chopped pecans.
- **Lunch** 5oz hamburger, a medium tomato, an avocado,1oz of cheddar cheese and 2 small Bibb lettuce leaves.
- **Snacks** Atkins friendly Creamy Lemon Smoothie; 2tbsp of green goddess dressing and ½ cup of chopped green bell pepper with 1oz of feta cheese.
- **Dinner** 6oz whitefish with ¼ cup of lentils, 1tbsp of butter and 1cup of green beans.

Day 5

- **Breakfast** Atkins friendly Frozen Farmhouse Style Scramble of sausages.
- **Lunch** 6oz Atkins turkey cutlets, 1tbsp of butter, 2cups of mixed greens, ½ cup of sliced bell pepper, ½ cup of sliced cucumber and 2 tbsp of raspberry vinaigrette
- **Snacks** 2 celery stalks with 2 tbsp of feta-ranch dressing, an ½ small apple and 2 oz of cheddar cheese.
- **Dinner** Atkins friendly Pork Chops With Fresh Mushrooms, a Bell Pepper and tomatoes with a ½ small baked potato, 2 tbsp of sour cream and 2 tbsp of butter.

Day 6

- **Breakfast** Atkins friendly Breakfast Mexi Peppers
- **Lunch** Cucumber, Tomato and Onion Salad With 4oz of turkey salami and a Creamy Feta Dressing.
- **Snacks** ½ cup of avocado and 2 tbsp of Greek vinaigrette; ½ cup of medium pear and 1oz of Brie cheese
- **Dinner** 6oz chicken, ¼ cup of brown rice, ¾ cup of stir-fry vegetables, 1tbsp of olive oil and 1tbsp of tamari sauce.

Day 7

- **Breakfast** Protein Pancakes with Double Chocolate.
- **Lunch** Snap Peas with Can Tuna, tomato, ½ of wheat pita and a Red Bell Pepper.
- **Snacks** Atkins Peanut Butter Crisp Bar with ¼ cup of hummus.
- **Dinner** Atkins friendly Beef Stroganoff

Here's what a week of eating could look like on the Atkins 100 diet.

Day 1

- **Breakfast** scrambled eggs with bacon, a tomato, green bell peppers and half a whole-wheat bagel.
- **Snacks** Atkins friendly White Chocolate Macadamia Nut Bar; small apple with 1oz of cheddar cheese
- **Lunch** Atkins friendly, Frozen Meat Lasagna with ½ cup of sliced cucumber, two cups of mixed greens, 5 cherry tomatoes and 1 cup of shredded carrot
- **Dinner** 2 cups of steamed broccoli with a Popcorn Garlic Shrimp, a cauliflower and ½ cup of brown rice.

Day 2

- **Breakfast** A small banana and a Milk Chocolate Protein Muffin
- **Lunch** A Cauliflower and Macaroni Salad with 5oz of hamburger, a whole-wheat bun, 2tbsp of onions and 2 tbsp of barbecue sauce.
- **Snacks** Atkins friendly, Mocha Latte Shake; ½ cup of strawberries with 4oz of plain unsweetened yogurt.
- **Dinner** 6oz of chicken breast, ¼ cup of chickpeas, 2tbsp of Cajun Rub, ¼ cup of baked acorn squash, 5 cherry tomatoes, 2 tbsp of Blue Cheese Dressing and 2 cups of mixed greens.

Day 3

- **Breakfast** Atkins friendly Farmhouse-Style Sausage Scramble with ½ cup of cubed honeydew melon.
- **Lunch** Atkins friendly Frozen Chicken Marsala with 2 cups of greens, ½ cup of sliced red bell pepper and 2 tbsp of Parmesan Peppercorn Dressing
- **Snacks** Atkins friendly Dark Chocolate Royale Shake; 15 corn of tortilla chips with 4 tbsp of black bean dip.
- **Dinner** A small tomato, 6oz of flank steak, ¼ cup of shredded carrot, 2 tbsp of Barbecue Rub, a medium sweet potato, 2 cups of baby kale, and 2 tbsp of Maple-Dijon Dressing.

Day 4

- **Breakfast** Atkins friendly Frozen Ham and Cheese Omelet.
- **Lunch** Grilled Lime Chicken with Spinach Salad, Sweet Cherry Pie and Feta-Ranch Dressing.

- **Snacks** A large tomato with 4 tbsp of hummus, Atkins friendly Mocha Latte Shake with a small banana.
- **Dinner** Classic Coleslaw and Quick Barbecued Pork with ¼ of a whole acorn squash and a whole-wheat bun.

Day 5

- **Breakfast** French Toast Loaf with 10 pecan halves and ¼ cup of blueberries.
- **Lunch** Chicken Sandwich with salad, Walnuts and Grapes.
- **Snacks** Atkins friendly Peanut Butter Fudge Bar and a small apple, ½ medium cucumber and 4 tbsp of black bean dip.
- **Dinner** Atkins friendly Frozen Stone Fired Meat Pizza served with Almond-Cinnamon Meringues, 2 cups of mixed greens, ½ cup of sliced bell pepper, 2 tbsp of Garlic Ranch Dressing and 1 cup of chickpeas.

Day 6

- **Breakfast** Fresh Blueberry Sauce with Sour Cream Waffles.
- **Lunch** Atkins friendly Frozen Mexican style Vegetable and Chicken with ½ cup of wild rice.
- **Snacks** Atkins friendly, French Vanilla Shake; 1tbsp of cream cheese with ½ cup of whole-wheat bagel.
- **Dinner** Fresh Guacamole and Fajita Steak with ¼ cup of Salsa Cruda, two 6-inch of corn tortillas and ¼ cup of black beans.

Day 7

- **Breakfast** ½ cup of blueberries and Protein Powered Oatmeal.
- **Lunch** Celery Salad and Daikon with 3.2 ounces of Italian sausage link, ½ cup of Basic Tomato Sauce and 1 cup of macaroni.
- **Snacks** Atkins Dark Chocolate Coconut Crunch Bar and a small tomato with ½ cup of cottage cheese
- **Dinner** Atkins friendly Frozen Chicken with ½ cup of peas and ¼ cup of brown rice.

3.6 Atkins-Friendly Snack Ideas:

One may consume balanced, low-carb snacks as well. In the Atkins diet, often people find it like their hunger is going down. They appear to be more than pleased with three meals a day (sometimes only 2).

If you feel hungry later, however, here are a few quick, healthy snacks:

- A hard-boiled egg or two.
- Leftovers.
- A piece of meat.
- Berries and whipped cream.
- Fruits (after induction)
- A handful of nuts.
- Some Greek yogurt.
- A piece of cheese.
- Baby carrots (careful during induction).

If you are on the Atkins 20 diet, you can choose these snacks such as:

- Crab dip with vegetables
- Smoked salmon, cucumber, and cream cheese roll-ups
- Black olives with cheddar
- Kale chips
- Cucumber guacamole

If you are on the Atkins 40 diet plan, you can have any snacks such as:

- A slice of whole-grain toast with almond butter
- Hummus
- ¾ cup of blackberries
- Greek yogurt

If the regular net carbohydrates may not reach 100 g, the Atkins 100 plan   followers can have any snacks.

You can steadily put back healthy carbs after induction is completed:

The Atkins diet is quite versatile, considering what you might have heard. You need to limit the consumption of carb sources only during the two-week induction process. After induction is done, nutritious carbohydrates such as higher-carb tomatoes, fruits, nuts, legumes, potatoes, and healthy grains such as oats and rice may be progressively added. However, even though you meet your weight reduction targets, chances are you may need to remain moderately low carb for life. You will gain the weight back if you resume consuming the same old things again in the same proportions as before. This is true in every plan for weight reduction.

3.7 What About Vegetarians?

Yeah, vegetarians and vegans can adopt the Atkins diet, but it would be more challenging to reach protein targets since certain go-to protein options are off-limits, such as seafood and beef (and milk for vegans). For all vegetarians and vegans, Atkins provides example menu plans and recipes, including carb totals.

If you are a vegetarian or vegan, you are going to start with extra carbs. In phase 2, vegetarians are given an additional handful, whereas vegans get about twice the normal amount of phase 2. (This is to get adequate nutrients from diets that could be more carb-heavy, in the absence of animal protein.) Most of your nutrition may have to come from plant sources (some vegetarians may even include eggs to make it easier), and you may need to include certain oils to boost your fat intake.

Researchers in Toronto created the Eco Atkins diet. 31 percent of calories come from (soy protein, eggs, tofu for vegetarians, veggie burgers for vegans, nuts, and cheese), 43 percent fat comes from (olive oil, avocado, and nuts), and 26 percent of the carbs from (fruit, vegetables, and whole grains). Small research conducted by BMJ Open in February 2014 showed that people lost around 15 lb. on the vegan version of the Eco Atkins diet after six months.

A multivitamin and a fish oil supplement (or flax oil for vegans) can both be used by vegans and vegetarians on the Atkins diet to guarantee that they receive sufficient amounts of nutrients. It is also advised that those on a diet leap straight onto Atkins 20 phase 2 or Atkins 40 as the Eco Atkins version's induction phase may be quite challenging. For Atkins, there is no need to add salt to all recipes. Stay well away from processed and dried foods as soon as you can, as sugar, other carbs and salt are sometimes added to them, which are bad for you.

Atkins does not require meat to be consumed by you. You are just going to have to skip the first phase of Atkins 20, which is too restricted to carbohydrates.

Vegetarians can get protein from:

- Eggs

- Eggs

- Nuts

- Legumes

- Cheese

- Soy

- Seeds

- High-protein grains like quinoa

Vegans can get protein from:

- Soy

- Nuts

- Legumes

- High-protein grains like quinoa

- Seeds

As a vegetarian (and vegan), it is possible to do the Atkins diet, however difficult. You should consume lots of nuts and seeds and use soy-based foods for protein. Excellent plant-based fat forms are olive oil and coconut oil. Lacto-ovo-vegetarians could also consume eggs, cheese, bacon, other high-fat dairy, and heavy cream.

Chapter 4: Easy To Make Recipes At Home:

The following are 7 Low-Carb Recipes in Under 10 Minutes:

The recipes below are easily prepared in less than 10 minutes, ideal for a busy, low-carb lifestyle at Atkins. There can be several health benefits from a low-carb Atkins diet, but you can struggle to create menu ideas that suit your busy schedule. It is simple to create delicious, low-carb meals that take less than 10 minutes of cooking time, even though you are not the most creative individual in the kitchen and have a few items at hand. All these meals are low-carb and friendly for weight loss.

- **Vegetables and Eggs Fried in Coconut Oil:**

This meal offers a perfect breakfast for you to enjoy every day. It is abundant in nutritious veggies and protein and leaves you satisfied for a long period.

Ingredients: Fresh vegetables or a combination of frozen vegetables (carrots, broccoli, cauliflower, green beans), spices, eggs, spinach (optional) and coconut oil.

The instructions:

1. In the frying pan, add some coconut oil and turn on the heat.

2. Only add vegetables. Let the vegetables defrost in the heat for a couple of minutes if you have a frozen mixture.

3. Put in 3-4 eggs.

4. Add the seasoning, either a mixture of spices or only salt and black pepper.

5. Now add some spinach (optional).

6. Stir-fry until prepared.

- **Grilled Chicken Wings served With Salsa and Greens:**

One of your favorites might just become this one. It needs little preparation because most people prefer to eat meat right from the bone. You might also find it meets the approval of your child.

Ingredients: Wings of chicken, peppers, salsa, greens.

The instructions:

1. In a seasoning mix of your choice, rub the chicken wings.

2. Put them in the microwave and heat them for around 40 minutes at 360-395 °F (180-200 °C).

3. Grill until the wings become crunchy and brown.

4. Serve with salsa and some greens.

- **Eggs and Bacon:**

Although bacon is a meat that has been processed and is not exactly nutritious, it is low in carbs. In a low-carb diet, you can eat it and yet lose weight. There is nothing wrong with incorporating it into your diet if you maintain your bacon consumption in balance and do not consume it more than once or twice a week.

Ingredients:

Milk, pork, spices (optional).

The instructions:

1. In a pan, add bacon and fry until ready.

2. Place the bacon and fried 3-4 eggs in the bacon fat on a pan.

3. Put a little garlic powder, onion powder and some sea salt on them when cooking if you want to give more spice to your eggs.

- **Ground Beef With thick slices of Bell Peppers**:

If you have some spare ground beef lying about, this low-carb meal is great.

Ingredients: coconut oil, ground beef, onion, herbs, bell pepper and spinach.

The instructions:

1. Chop the onion finely.

2. In a pan, add coconut oil and turn up the stove.

3. Add some onion, then stir for a minute or two.

4. Add some ground beef.

5. Add any of the ingredients, like a mix or just salt and pepper.

6. Now add some spinach.

7. You may add some black pepper and chili flakes if you like to spice it up a little.

8. Stir-fry and serve with sliced bell pepper when prepared.

- **Cheeseburgers without buns:**

A bun less burger with two different types of cheese and a side of fresh spinach does not get any better than this:

Ingredients: Cheddar cheese, butter, hamburger patties, cream cheese, salsa, seasoning, spinach.

The instructions:

1. In a pan, add butter and turn the heat on.

2. Now add the hamburger patties and seasoning.

3. Flip the patties until they are nearly ready.

4. On top, add a few cheddar slices and some cream cheese.

5. Reduce the heat before the cheese melts and place a cover on the pan.

6. With fresh spinach, serve it. If you prefer, you can simmer some of the fats from the pan over your greens.

7. Add some sauce to make the burgers much juicier.

- **Fried Chunks of a Chicken Breast:**

If you are nervous about ending up with distasteful, dry chicken and adding, some butter might be the trick.

Ingredients: butter, salt, chicken breast, spices, curry powder, garlic powder and leafy greens.

The instructions:

1. Cut the breast of the chicken into smaller pieces.

2. In a pan, add butter and turn the heat on.

3. Add pieces of chicken, salt, pepper, curry, and powdered garlic.

4. Brown the chicken till a crunchy appearance is reached.

5. Serve with some leafy vegetables.

- **Meatza, a combo of meat and pizza:**

If on a low-carb diet you miss pizza, then you are going to love it. Without the harmful additives that many pizza types contain, you can find that it tastes much better. This recipe is simple to change, and you can add tomatoes, mushrooms, various cheeses, and any low-carb ingredients you like.

Ingredients: Sausage, tomatoes, ground beef, salsa, sauces, powdered garlic, and shredded cheese.

The instructions:

1. Chop the onions finely and slice some of the bacon into thin strips.

2. At the bottom of the baking dish, mix the ground beef, salsa, tomatoes, peppers, and garlic powder.

3. Sprinkle on top with melted cheese and layer with extra strips of bacon.

4. Put in the oven and heat for 30 to 40 minutes at 360 to 395 ° F (180 to 200 ° C) before the bacon and cheese look crunchy.

Chapter 5: Eating Out And Shopping With Atkins Plan:

It is entirely feasible to adhere to the diet when eating out with just a little planning. It is not important to eat organic, and always go with the least refined choice that suits the budget.

5.1 How to Follow the Atkins Diet When Eating Out:

Only because you are living a low-carb lifestyle does not imply that you need to avoid eating out to dinner every once and a while!

Ultimately, the safest diet for weight loss and other health issues is the one that a person practices to reach and sustain healthier body weight, so the Atkins diet is a strong and productive way to lose weight and stay healthy at the end of the day. You are not going to be disappointed.

When you think of beginning a low-carb weight loss diet, several people believe that it will eventually become a thing of the past to indulge in delicious food at their favorite restaurant. Not too easily! It can be just as simple, pleasant, and satisfying to eat out when on Atkins as before. Before you go out to dinner, consuming a light snack can help keep you from overeating at the restaurant. Pick food that is nutritious and filling, like vegetables and guacamole or a few turkey or ham roll-ups, but it will not ruin your appetite.

First, consider the genre of cuisine as you pick a restaurant. "Choose a restaurant that will serve more protein-based dishes than an Italian restaurant, such as an American restaurant," stated Rebecca Guterman, RD, a clinical dietitian at New York City's Mount Sinai Hospital. Before you arrive, check the menu online so you can plot your order in advance. Look for recipes that rely on lean meats and veggies. A salad served with grilled chicken or a burger without a bun, and a side salad is a decent choice. In place of bread, rice or potatoes, some suggestions include getting extra veggies. Order a meal typically based on fatty meat or fish that is fatty. With your meal, get some extra sauce, butter, or olive oil.

Usually, implementing the Atkins diet at most restaurants is simple.

- **Start with salads:** Be conscious of the salad's ingredients; do not buy salads that come in a shell (such as taco salad) and go easy on add-ins like coleslaw and strips of tortilla. Also, make sure that every meat you get is grilled, not breaded, with your salad. When you are in the early stages of a low carb diet, fruits such as grapes and mango higher in carbohydrates are often avoided.

    Vegetables are low in net carbs and filled with fiber, ensuring that every meal is a perfect start. "Before your main entrance, always have a salad first, with greens and you will stop over doing it." Monica Patino lost about 46 pounds on Atkins.

- **Bring your own dressings with you:** Many people carry their favorite spices or small bottles of hot sauce with them, and when they eat out, spice their restaurant meals as desired. Take your sauce with you with your salad anytime you head out to a restaurant because you know just how much carbohydrates **you receive. Only take an old bottle and fill it in your purse** or pocket with your favorite dressing. Yeah, you might get an odd look, but it is worth the looks you will get when you are slim, stated Terry Elkins, who lost 103 pounds on the Atkins diet.

- **You know your triggers so try to avoid them.** Make a strategy in advance for how to prevent your meal from potential carb-filled pitfalls. And stick with that. "Dining out at Atkins is so convenient. You know what you should have right now and what a food trigger is. Do not feel guilty calling for broccoli or Brussels sprouts to supplement the fries or potatoes. I tell continuously,' Kindly keep the croutons.' You have got to do what you have got to do.' Stated Andrea Morgan, who lost 105 pounds on Atkins diet plan.

- **Request a substitute:** Restaurants are in the business of providing service. One can be more than able to satisfy most demands, as long as you are respectful to the server. Do not be afraid to inquire about replacing things or getting it made as you like it when you dine out! Instead of fries or extra vegetables, I still ask for a salad in place of chips or pasta. Many restaurants can satisfy the order of a customer! Stated Emelie Jurgens (Lost 89 pounds). Several restaurants give free bread or baskets of tortilla chips to start the lunch. If you have a hard time avoiding the break basket temptation, kindly inform the server that you do not require the basket or inquire if necessary, for them to take that away earlier than usual. If salsa, hummus, or guacamole arrives with bread or chips comes with hummus, salsa, or guacamole, ask for its replacement.

- **Master the art of fast food: Due to crazy job schedules, after-school activities and more, you can find yourselves at the fast-food drive-thru more regularly** than you want. Cut back on your fast-food visits is not a bad idea, but if you go, there are choices. With respect to dining out, I have three little children who enjoy fast food. I have grown to enjoy Wendy's because they have no difficulty making a double hamburger without even a bun and encouraging me to replace French fries with a Caesar side salad. "My children remain happy, and I can stick to my plan." stated Randy Fisher who Lost 80 pounds while following Atkins diet.

- **Stay hydrated:** Often, hunger will stimulate thirst. And even a quick snack would also quench some food, causing hunger pangs until you head out to dinner. Grab and consume a huge quantity of water and get a string of cheese or unsalted walnuts or peanuts. Still remember the nutritious quality and fiber, but 2 to 4 net carbs are present in certain mini low-carb nuts. Cheryl Lynn Wolf appeared to have lost 50 pounds on Atkins diet.

- **Be adventurous:** Get creative with the restaurant menu and choose fresh low-carb items that you might never have eaten before. We still ride a fair deal, and that is when you choose to make your food options more adventurous. You can truly enjoy a grilled rack of lamb at a restaurant. It is better to pick the lower-carb options rather than a higher carb kind of bread, for example, whole-wheat bread. Such items as gravy are generally avoided and should be extremely careful about sauces, but you must trust that it is the best choice.

At some famous restaurants, here are a few low-carb dishes you can try:

- ✓ **Chili's** Chicken or Steak Fajitas without tortillas and toppings and with a double serving of vegetables instead of rice.
- ✓ **Olive Garden** Herb-Grilled Salmon with Parmesan garlic broccoli on the side
- ✓ **The Cheesecake Factory** Pan Seared Branzino with Lemon Butter
- ✓ **P.F. Chang's** Shrimp with Lobster Sauce
- ✓ **Butternut Squash Noodles** All you need is a little parmesan and olive oil on top.
- ✓ **Antipasto-Stuffed Chicken** This super simple chicken dinner can boast an absolute knock out of flavor.
- ✓ **Burrito Zucchini Boat:** Less carbs but more meat.
- ✓ **Zucchini Lasagna Roll-Ups** Your low-carb lasagna dreams have come true.
- ✓ **Mashed Cauliflower** You will not even miss the potatoes.
- ✓ **Taco Tomatoes** These are the prettiest low-carb tacos you will ever see.
- ✓ **Zucchini Sushi** These little bites are super refreshing.
- ✓ **Low-Carb Pot Pies** Rice with cauliflower makes a healthier pot pie crust.

- ✓ **Caprese Zoodles** The Caprese salad your life has been missing.
- ✓ **Chicken Parm Stuffed Peppers** There's no wrong way to eat chicken parm...but do try this way as well.
- ✓ **Eggplant Lasagna** This is the vegetarian lasagna you have been searching for.
- ✓ **Cheesesteak Stuffed Peppers** A Philly favorite with a twist!
- ✓ **Grilled Cabbage "Steaks"** These will let you think about cabbage in a whole new light.
- ✓ **Beef Zucchini Enchiladas** Low-carb enchiladas for the win!
- ✓ **Low-Carb Big Macs** The guilt free way to enjoy your favorite hamburger.
- ✓ **Zuddha Bowls** A low carb Buddha Bowl!

Avoid including condiments in the meal and go for extra veggies or side salad over a starchy side (honey, mustard, barbecue sauce and ketchup are cunningly high in carbs).

5.2 A Basic Atkins diet simple shopping list to follow:

Shopping on the perimeter of the store is a safe rule. This is a place typically where all the food is usually available.

If you are preparing a diet for Atkins 20, Atkins 40 or Atkins 100, here are some important foods that you will need to buy:

- ✓ **Proteins,** including whitefish, chicken, pork chops, ground beef and salmon.
- ✓ **Vegetables** like broccoli, cauliflower, radishes, tomatoes, spinach, cauliflower, kale, lettuce, asparagus, onions, mushrooms etc.
- ✓ **Fats** like olive oil, butter, coconut oil and extra virgin olive oil.
- ✓ **Fruits** like pears, apples, oranges, and avocados.
- ✓ **Full-fat dairy products** like cheddar cheese, Greek yogurt, eggs, dressing of blue cheese, cream, eggs, and Greek yogurt.
- ✓ **Fatty fish:** Trout, salmon etc.
- ✓ **Shellfish and Shrimp**.
- ✓ **Nuts:** Almonds, walnuts, macadamia nuts, hazelnuts, etc.
- ✓ **Seeds:** Pumpkin seeds, sunflower seeds etc.
- ✓ **Condiments:** Turmeric, pepper, garlic, cinnamon, parsley, sea salt etc.

  In the Atkins shopping list to adopt, the descriptions of certain widely valued nutritional products suggested by some nutritionists are:

✓ **Eggs**

Compared to other diet plans, the Atkins diet embraces the whole egg that promotes low-fat egg whites as a protein-rich breakfast choice. That is because the yolk offers the body the requisite fats for the plan to run properly. slice half an avocado, drizzle extra virgin oil, add a sprinkle of sea salt, and then add a fried egg on top," says Dr. Cohen. "It is tasty, healthy, and simple. The mixture of good fats and protein convert it into a satisfying meal.

✓ **Leafy greens**

"I'll eat all the greens for lunch, and lots of them," Dr. Cohen says. "My favorite is Arugula." Spinach and kale, since they are rich in vitamins C, k and A, and other nutrients, both are good options. So, eat as much as you can; these leafy greens are the best choice.

✓ **Cucumbers**

Cucumber is technically a fruit, quite low in calories and a strong water quality, which tends to fill a person up. Eat cucumbers as a snack or as a topping for salads. The seeds can also be scooped out and you can make cucumber boats loaded with your favorite topping approved by Atkins. Notice when you quit eating carbohydrates, what happens to the body.

✓ **Salmon**

Trader Joe's provides wild, already cooked Pacific salmon. Throughout the day, I will select this or flake it on top of a salad,' says Dr. Cohen. Salmon is rich in omega-3 fatty acids and proteins, and you can get the extra value of calcium from the edible if you prefer the canned one.

✓ **Peppers**

Bell peppers are rich in fiber and vitamins. Stuff these peppers with a mix of cooked protein, such as pork or chicken, and vegetables, like onions, greens, garlic, or fresh herbs, to make an Atkins-approved meal. Then bake them in an oven with virgin olive oil sauteed on top of them.

✓ **Beef**

While several low-calorie diets reject beef for leaner chicken or turkey, its higher fat content is accepted by the Atkins diet. "I like to get grass-fed beef and make a creative side dish with butter and sea salt, like mashed cauliflower," Dr. Cohen says.

✓ **Tuna**

Tuna is rich in protein and healthy fats, whether fresh or canned, making it one of the most enjoyable Atkins diet products. "Once a week, I will make canned chunk of light tuna-it has less mercury than white tuna," says Dr. Cohen. Dollop it on the lettuce, or dip it in with celery sticks, carrots, cucumber, or other favorite veggies.

✓ **Pickles**

Pickles are a perfect Atkins snack; before purchasing, be sure to review the sugar and salt quality. " Do not buy butter and bread pickles. They are soaked in sugar," says Dr. Cohen,

✓ **Chia seeds**

Chia seeds, tiny but strong, are a gold mine of protein, fiber, and healthy fat. They also create a balanced dessert that is Atkins-approved. "Chia seeds, half-and-a-half, monk-fruit sweetener, and some blueberries make pudding," Dr. Cohen states. The fats and proteins supply a sweet tooth with a satiating solution.

✓ **Cheese**

Yeah, cheese is listed in Atkins diet foods; moderation is the key. "I'm going to buy tons of veggies and make a huge salad with some protein and a little cheese on top," Dr. Cohen says. The particularly great option is blue cheese: it is so flavorful; you need a light sprinkling for a big flavor effect. Learn why these high-carb foods will ruin your health if you do not avoid consuming them.

✓ **Avocado**

You will also eat your favorite green fruit on the Atkins diet, Dr. Cohen assures you. Rejoice, avocado lovers. Healthy mono- and poly-unsaturated fats are filled in avocados that make you stay feeling full and balance blood sugar levels.

✓ **Asparagus**

Asparagus is a non-starchy vegetable, ensuring it will not add many net carbohydrates each day to your total. For a tasty side dish or salad topping, sauté it with garlic, extra virgin olive oil, lemon juice, salt, and pepper. These are the things consumed all the time by skinny people.

✓ **Broccoli**

Cruciferous vegetables such as broccoli, Dr. Cohen notes, are rich in fiber and low in carbohydrates, making them a better option for Atkins' diet foods. In the oven, bake them, or in a salad, add them raw to make your meal a satisfying one.

✓ **Full-fat dairy**

Load up on tofu and cottage cheese that are full in fat. You could also have whipped cream. "Berries are a good dessert with real whipped cream," says Dr. Cohen. Do not skip these other little improvements to your diet that will help you lose weight.

Clearing the pantry with all harmful items and products is strongly encouraged. It involves ice cream, bread, soda, beverages and baking products such as sugar and wheat flour and breakfast cereals.

Chapter 6: Typical Results:

Over the years, the Atkins diet plan has passed through several adjustments. There are several variables in the strict diet schedule that you can remember before implementing it. Atkins presents many advantages that may render it the best diet for others. But the disadvantages could rule it out for others. Whether you are considering this plan to lose weight for better, before you initiate the diet, make sure that you analyze both the pros and cons of Atkins.

THE PROS & CONS OF ATKINS DIET

6.1 Pros and Cons:

The diet works on the idea that weight gain is induced by the metabolism of carbohydrates, particularly refined and starchy carbs such as wheat, potatoes, or pasta, not by fat consumption or food proportions, but by how our body system interacts the breakdown. The Atkins Diet includes a maintenance regimen for the first couple of weeks, which requires the incremental re-introduction of certain carbs into the diet to sustain weight loss. Even at this point, the carb consumption is far lower than most people are used to.

This diet can be quite challenging throughout the initial phase - especially for individuals who are used to large amounts of carbohydrates in their everyday diets. There can be a wide range of side effects from the dramatic fall in carb intake. Common ones are nausea, dizziness, migraines, and faintness in the first few days. Poor breath, triggered by the body heading through ketosis, is another somewhat unpleasant side-effect. For those who enjoy the thought of a fry-up each morning, The Atkins Diet is great. Eggs, pancakes, sausage, Baked, baked, grilled. It does not matter - on this diet, all of them are recommended. There are also very low to no carb ingredients in cheese, butter, and milk, and they are also advised on this diet. So, what do these topics all have in common? All of them are heavy in saturated fat, dieters are also cautious of whether it is appropriate to fill their bodies full of too much saturated fatty content.

There are also advantages and drawbacks of the Atkins Diet, as in other diets. This diet encourages accelerated weight reduction and requires dieters to ingest limitless fatty and protein-rich foods. This Atkins diet has also been found to not be as time-consuming and costly as some other common diets.

The Atkins Diet states that during the first two weeks of step 1, you will drop 15 pounds (6.8 kilograms), but it also admits that those are not standard outcomes. The Atkins Diet also admits that you will initially lose weight with liquids. It states that in phases 2 and 3, you can begin to lose weight as long as you are not eating more calories than your body will handle.

The Atkins diet will help an individual lose weight. For several, it would often lower the likelihood of type 2 diabetes, heart disease and would often lower other forms of metabolic syndrome by losing weight. Most people will lose weight, at least in the short term, with virtually every diet plan that limits calories. However, in the long run, findings indicate that low-carb diets such as the Atkins Diet are not any more successful than traditional weight-loss diets for weight loss and that, regardless of diet schedule, most individuals recover the weight they lose.

The primary explanation for weight reduction on the Atkins Diet is lower average calorie consumption by consuming fewer carbs because carbohydrates typically supply more than half of the calories eaten. Any reports indicate that the Atkins Diet has other causes for weight loss. Although the extra fat and protein keep you staying full longer, you will lose pounds, so your food options are reduced, and you consume less. These two effects lead to lower average consumption of calories.

PROS:

Weight Loss	Up to 15 pounds in the first two weeks (including water weight).	water
Food	Low-carbohydrates, high-fat commercial plan.	
A healthy Heart	May lower blood pressure, raise good cholesterol.	

It may be a perfect way to drop more weight and improve the overall health to follow a diet, but there are more precise factors why everyone chooses a diet. That can include decreasing blood pressure or cholesterol levels, minimizing the risk for heart disease, or increasing energy levels. A handful of possible pros are available to follow the Atkins food schedule.

LOW CALORIE/ HIGH CARB DIET   VS   ATKINS

UP AND DOWN SUGAR LEVELS

STEADY SUGAR LEVELS

INCREASED
• FAT STORAGE
• HUNGER/CRAVINGS

LESS
• FAT STORAGE
• HUNGER/CRAVINGS

BURN SUGAR/ STORE FAT

BURN FAT/ LOSE WEIGHT

For one, the diet is reasonably simple to stick to. Richard D. Feinman, Ph.D., a biochemistry professor at the State University of New York Downstate Medical Center in Brooklyn, New York, and the publisher and former co-editor in chief of the journal Nutrition & Metabolism, argues that a carbohydrate-restricted diet minimizes this fight. Any meal is a fight for people who struggle with weight, a serious psychological burden. Clinical trials on Atkins and diets restricted to carbohydrates were performed by Dr. Feinman. The secure part of the diet is the protein that will give you more control over the war on food.

The diet is also not based on managing portions used in typical diets by certain individuals as a challenge. What does the regulation of portions mean? Self-control, because there's no good record for it,' Feinman notes. Small servings are great, so if you are still starving, you can eat another small portion with a low-carbohydrate diet. You will be out of luck on a low-fat diet if you are still hungry.

Susan Kraus, RD, a professional dietitian at Hackensack University Medical Center in New Jersey, says the Atkins diet's simple form would make it simpler for some people to adhere to it. "People feel it is easy to follow." she says, "You focus on a few food groups, you have flexibility in that you do not have to calculate food, and you do not feel deprived."

By following the low-carb fad diet, individuals with type 2 diabetes aiming for a solution for elevated blood pressure will also be helped. Reducing carbohydrates, either you lose the weight or not, has a health advantage. For example, a January 2015 report in Diet suggests that lowering carbohydrates can help treat diabetes and metabolic syndrome. If you participate in the Atkins diet, there is detailed literature documenting the consequences of focusing on a low-carb diet. Many of these published findings have confirmed the usage of the plan for weight loss and other health benefits.

The Atkins Diet claims that its dietary regimen will avoid or improve severe health conditions, along with metabolic syndrome, diabetes, blood pressure or heart failure. Almost any diet that helps you shed excess weight can minimize heart disease and diabetes risk factors or even reverse them.

Weight Loss:

There is a fine record of effective weight reduction on the Atkins diet. Many individuals on this initiative have lost weight, and the method has been tested in several clinical studies. But you can find that there are many trials with contradictory results whether you recommend Atkins for weight reduction or weight management.

An examination of findings conducted in the journal Nutrients contrasted Atkins to 19 different diets without clear expectations for calories.1 The researchers noticed that the Atkins diet showed the best proof of the examined diets in achieving clinically beneficial short-term and long-term weight reduction.

For two years, a further analysis conducted in the Annals of Internal Medicine examined 307 people. For two years, participants adopted either a low-fat diet or a low-carbohydrate nutrition program described in Dr. Atkins' New Diet Revolution. The study authors noticed that when combined with behavioral therapy, both programs could achieve substantial weight loss, but the low-carbohydrate approach was correlated with positive improvements in risk factors for cardiovascular disease.

However, there is still an extensive study that compared high-fat ketogenic diets (like Atkins) to diets where there are limited calories. Many of these experiments have found that there is little distinction between calorie reduction and carb restriction for long-term weight reduction. Besides, while there is some encouragement for low-carbohydrate, higher fat diets, medical researchers are also debating whether the plan is safe for the long-term.

You may have chosen to start Atkins because you needed to lose weight, but did you realize that study has found that a low-carb diet like Atkins has shown far other advantages in 'off label' that only lose weight? These contain, to name a few: epilepsy and associated disorders, acid reflux (GERD), acne, headache, cardiac failure, cancer, polycystic ovary syndrome (PCOS), insulin resistance/diabetes/metabolic syndrome, dementia, and narcolepsy.

Epilepsy:

In certain patients on one or more antiepileptic medications, epilepsy is a debilitating and common neurological condition that can successfully manage. About 30 percent of people with seizures have refractory epilepsy, and correctly selected and utilized antiepileptic drug schedules have failed sufficient studies to induce prolonged relief of epilepsy.

More than 30 reports from 2004 to 2014 endorse the usage of a Modified Atkins Diet in adults and adolescents to better relieve the effects of epilepsy and associated seizure disorders. This has been extremely promising for children living with childhood epilepsy who do not respond to medication for seizure control.

A high-fat, low-protein, and carbohydrate diet, with few calories and fluids, consisting of the traditional Atkins diet, is a promising diet plan. The Atkins diet is a therapeutic modality that has been used as a treatment for intractable epilepsy since the 1920s. It has been suggested as a dietary therapy, which is already documented in the Hippocratic collection, that would produce similar fasting advantages. The Atkins diet is rich in fat and has minimal protein and carbohydrate content. Information suggests that for non-surgical Pharmacoresistant epilepsy patients of any generation, KD and its derivatives are a suitable choice, considering that the form of diet should be individually designed, and that less restrictive and more palatable diets are often safer choices for adults and teenagers. This analysis addresses the Atkins diet, including potential modes of action, applicability, side effects, and proof of its success and more palatable diets in children and adults, such as Low Glycemic index Diet (LGID) and the Modified Atkins Diet (MAD).

Control Diabetes: Although most diets will help to overcome a broad variety of health conditions, the Atkins diet is the only option in our world today to address a particular and common medical problem: diabetes. 25.8 million persons in the United States (8.3 percent of the population) have diabetic issues, and 79 million individuals have pre-diabetes, as per the American Diabetes Association. This is a challenge that needs to be addressed seriously, with so many individuals now at risk for diabetes and the pace at which diagnosed cases are growing. Weight reduction is one of the most key parameters of managing diabetes or maintaining health for a diabetic individual, and the Atkins diet is a perfect way to do this. The Atkins Diet is an excellent way to keep it from progressing, particularly though you do not have diabetes. Insulin resistance, or when their glucose levels do not want to go down, is what challenges certain individuals with type 2 diabetes. The trouble with insulin resistance is that the body system is slow to respond to the medication most likely to benefit it. This tolerance contributes to elevated insulin levels being prescribed to diabetics, and weight gain is a side effect of a high-level insulin treatment because insulin accelerates fat accumulation and synthesis. In brief, the harder someone do efforts to regulate their blood sugar level with insulin, the most possible it is for them to add weight.

What made the Atkins diet the best diabetic diet is that the amount of carbohydrates eaten is limited as the Atkins diet reduces the number of carbs consumed by a person. Although lowering calories can usually contribute to weight reduction, diabetic medications also cause side effects and appetite stimulation, rendering it impossible to lose weight on a normal diet.

Studies have shown that a low-carb diet will significantly increase blood glucose regulation and blood lipids for individuals with type 2 diabetes. These results are important since they offer a means for people with diabetes to minimize their obesity and treat their diabetes.

When you exclude added sugar and reduce the carb consumption to primarily 'foundation vegetables' while on the Atkins diet, insulin tolerance increases along with blood glucose regulation. Under the guidance of a specialist, several individuals who mainly eat foundation vegetables may notice that they will avoid or decrease their dependency on blood-sugar-lowering medicines. Before you are using Atkins, you can work very closely with the doctor to change the dosage. The need for medicine that reduces blood sugar would decline easily.

With your health and nutrition, one should be careful. There are tons of foods for diabetes, but the safest diabetes plan is the Atkins diet. If you have diabetes, or you are at risk of diabetes or wish to boost your overall health and lose weight, a perfect way to improve your health is to turn to the low carb Atkins diet and then focus on this healthy carbs diet.

The Atkins diet excludes processed carbohydrates like baked goods (such as cake and white bread) and supports the consumption of healthier carbohydrates, particularly in the later stages of the diet (such as green vegetables and berries rich in fiber). And you will understand the distinction between good and bad carbohydrates.

Simply lowering the consumption of processed grains and sugary drinks offers noticeable advantages for multiple individuals straight away. Instead of soda, consuming water and replacing starchy dishes with foundation vegetables are sure to benefit you, and you will have steady levels of energy during the day. Additionally, once you scale down on your carb consumption, you can drop water weight relatively quickly.

A healthy heart:

Between 2002 and 2014, twenty-one studies examined the function of low-carb diets and how they may help reduce risk factors for cardiac disease and chances for depression and stroke. It has been demonstrated that the usage of a low-carb diet not only assists with weight control but often increases blood pressure, levels of cholesterol and triglycerides and reduces inflammation, these factors correlated with cardiac disease.

It is a sobering fact that the number one killer among Americans is heart failure. It is a vital opportunity to make sure you are doing all you can to keep yourself safe because February is American Heart Month. Any literature shows that Atkins improves healthy HDL cholesterol and reduces blood pressure, lowering the likelihood of stroke and heart disease. All that fat, though, scares most specialists. Some health professionals suggest that, as permitted on the Atkins Diet, consuming a significant amount of protein fat from animal sources can raise the risk of heart disease or some cancers, but thankfully, evidence continues to show that individuals who adopt a controlled-carb, higher-fat eating plan such as Atkins (which does not contain trans fats) typically have better amounts of 'good' HDL cholesterol and the lower number of triglycerides. They often lost more weight than people who adopted a standard low-fat diet. Some fats are healthy for your heart, and they are essential components of Atkins, too. These fats include monounsaturated fats in almonds, avocados, olive oil, canola oil, and polyunsaturated fats found in seafood, soybeans, sunflower seeds and flaxseeds, and cottonseed, safflower oil and maize. Try to have fatty cold-water fish such as salmon, halibut, and tuna, high in omega-3 fatty acids, for at least two servings a week (3.5 ounces). Omega 3s can decrease triglycerides, slow down the atherosclerotic plaque rate, and lower blood pressure.

Cancer:

Obesity is a cause correlated with the elevated incidence of certain cancers, but a low-carb diet is seen to help people reduce weight and sustain their weight loss. It has a beneficial influence on lowering the risk of some cancers. an Examples involve results from a 2012 report in the Journal of National Cancer Institute indicating that higher average consumption of carbohydrates and higher dietary glycemic load is correlated with a high risk of recurrence and mortality in colon cancer in stage III, which suggests that a low-carb diet (which is super low glycemic) could help improve colon cancer survival rates. Another Nutrition and Cancer (2010) research found that a low-carb diet helps overweight women who are survivors of breast cancer reduce weight, lowering their likelihood of cardiac failure and other obesity-related illnesses, as well as breast cancer recurrence.

PCOS:

The most prevalent endocrine disease impacting women of reproductive age is polycystic ovary syndrome (PCOS) and is correlated with obesity, insulin resistance and hyperinsulinemia. since low carbohydrate diets have been shown to decrease insulin resistance, examined the six-month endocrine and metabolic effects of a low-carbohydrate, keto diet (LCKD) on overweight or obese women with PCOS in a pilot study (Nutrition and Metabolism, 2005). In this pilot study, in women with obesity and PCOS over 24 weeks, LCKD contributed to substantial changes in weight, LH/FSH ratio, percent free testosterone and fasting insulin. Another 2004 pilot analysis saw related promising findings in the Journal of General Internal Medicine showing resistance to Diabetes/Metabolic Syndrome/Insulin. Twenty-nine reports, going back to 1998, indicate that low-carb diets significantly reduce the effects and complications of diabetes, metabolic syndrome, and resistance to insulin.

No Calorie Counting:

Frustration with the use of counting calories for weight reduction and weight management is increasing. While most fitness experts understand the value of eating the correct number of calories per day, they recognize that it may be boring and restrictive to attempt and track and control your consumption every day.

You track the Atkins plan's net carb consumption, so there is no requirement for calories to be counted or restricted. This aspect of the Atkins plan is the most attractive to many individuals.

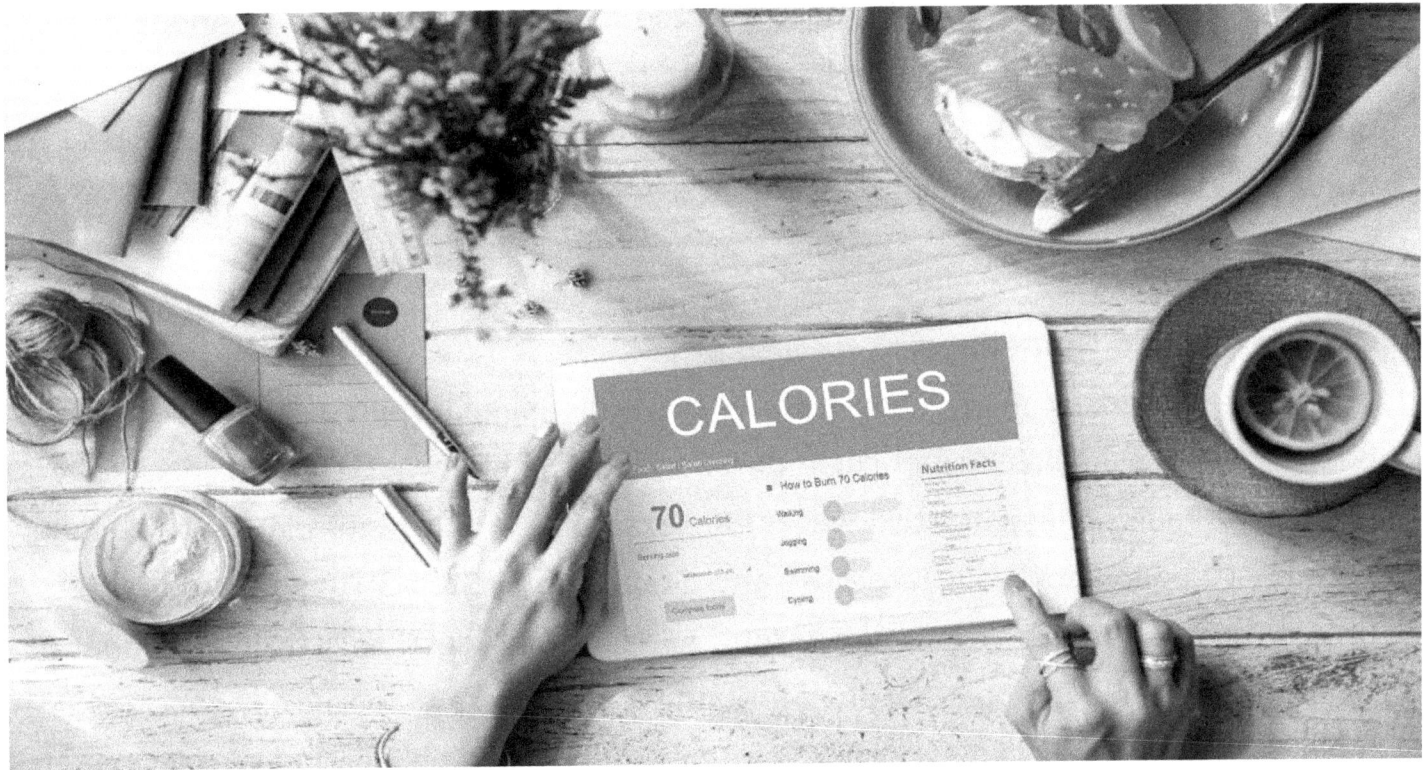

Hearty Eating Plan:

Some people enjoy the idea that you will consume richer and fulfilling food on the Atkins diet schedule. Some may choose this diet, for instance, so hearty foods such as steaks and burgers will remain on their plate.

Foods high in protein and foods containing more fat seem to be more enjoyable. You are likely to postpone the next meal or snack because you feel full after eating and can consume fewer calories overall as a consequence. Several tests have found that the Atkins strategy has a lower average calorie consumption than other programs with a higher intake of carbohydrates.

However, it is necessary to remember that the more recent versions of Atkins have portion size guidelines. E.g., for added fat, the daily recommended consumption during Phase 1 is only 2-4 tablespoons. So, if you eat huge portions of fatty beef, butter, and cheese, you cannot trust the Atkins plan to work.

Clearly Defined Guidelines:

Atkins is enjoyed by many people who want a disciplined approach to food. Each phase of the plan has a particular duration or weight target that is specifically explained. Phase 1 lasts for two weeks, for example (in most situations). Until you become 10 pounds off your target weight, Step 2 lasts. Step 3 runs for four weeks before you are safely at your target weight. At each point, detailed lists of appropriate foods are available, and portion sizes for and type of food are specifically specified.

Anyone who has practiced Atkins will inform you about the advantages of a low-carb lifestyle; here are few unexpected advantages of dieting Atkins.

1. Willpower strengthens.

one can say, when you first think about Atkins, "How can I live without ice cream or bread?" Or some high carb snack that people enjoy. This all changes while following Atkins after a week or two. The cravings disappear when the blood sugar normalizes. In reality, if you have a 'blip' and consume any high carb junk, then you start to know how it makes you feel bloated and hungry. Plus, you are discovering new favorite recipes that nourish the body without zapping the life out of it.

2. Tell goodbye to hunger.

As Atkins diet conjures up visions of countless plates of lettuce, egg white omelets or worse, nothing, one does not want to think of Atkins as a 'diet.' This low carb, high protein plan leaves you feeling happy.

The truth, though, remains that people are too full to eat, but the pounds are coming off, and they feel fine. The reasoning for this is that, of course, each Atkins meal is high in protein and dietary fat, so it is really enjoyable, and you feel nicely satisfied because you are not cutting back on calories.

3. One can feel more focused:

You send a kid a bag of candy, and just before your eyes, you can see them becoming hyper. When they jump off the wall on a sugar high, they find it hard to concentrate on one thing.

Well, if the body transitions to ketosis, the inverse happens. You realize your mental concentration significantly enhances. This is a great advantage to Atkins that most individuals appear to lower their carbohydrates in a week or 2.

4. Enhances Stamina:

You can expect to see a significant rise in strength levels on a low carb diet once you have finished the adaptation period to move to ketosis (approximately 1-2 weeks). You will be motivated to raise more weights or realize you have more stamina to keep up with the kids. Exercise would be much easier. This is because, for nutrition, the body adapts to burning fat. Because we have a far higher abundance of fat than carbohydrates, energy levels are soaring. However, if you notice that after two weeks on Atkins, you are deficient in energy, try increasing salt consumption. Atkins is usually a diuretic, suggesting that as the water retention reduces, you must replace the lost salt. However, do not worry; you do not consume fatty, processed foods on Atkins to lower your consumption.

5. Your mood is dramatically change:

You will find that you feel a lot brighter without the frequent peaks and drops of blood sugar that zap vitality and steal your mood. When it comes to mind, diet serves like therapy because, although you might have already consumed sugar foods while you were low, this goes against what you are trying to do and only makes you feel much more unhappy. You will balance your blood sugar with Atkins, bring a jump in your step and stop the sugary 'highs' and 'lows.'

Cons:

The Atkins Diet admits that, in the initial phase of the program, dramatically reducing carbs will result in several side effects, such as:

- Headache
- Weakness
- Fatigue
- Constipation
- Weakness
- Dizziness

Also, carbs are so reduced by certain very low carb diets that they result in dietary shortages or inadequate fiber, which may cause health concerns such as nausea, diarrhea, and constipation.

However, consuming high-fiber, full-grain, and nutrient-dense carbohydrates will boost the nutritional profile of the Atkins Diet's initiatives. In comparison, to better avoid health issues, the Atkins Diet has evolved, and it now advises consuming a moderate quantity of additional sodium, along with nutrients or supplements.

It is also likely that ketosis can limit carbs to less than 20 grams a day, the amount prescribed for phase 1 of the diet. When you have not enough sugar (glucose) for power, ketosis happens because your body breaks down accumulated fat, allowing your body to build up ketones. Nausea, headache, emotional exhaustion, and foul breath can be side effects of ketosis.

Moreover, the Atkins Diet is not ideal for all. For starters, whether you are taking diuretics, oral diabetes or insulin drugs, the Atkins Diet advises that you contact a doctor before beginning the diet. Furthermore, individuals with serious kidney failure do not adopt the diet, and diet stages of weight reduction are not necessary for breastfeeding and pregnant people.

Some individuals who come to Atkins attempt their first diet, some have tried several various diets, but they have never found the best match. Anyway, we agree that the basic but powerful ideals of a low-carb lifestyle will help everyone.

In 2019, at both the American Society of Diet and the Diabetes Association conferences, announced findings from a broad nutritional analysis. The results show that there is not a particular diet that satisfies the needs of any person attempting to lose weight since each body reacts differently. These results reinforce studies reported in other scientific papers that show that the diet you will adhere to for the long-term is the safest diet for weight loss. And most diets for weight reduction, not just low-carb diets, can, at least momentarily, increase blood cholesterol or blood glucose levels. One research found that triglycerides were enhanced by persons who adopted the Atkins Diet, indicating improved cardiac protection. But no big studies have demonstrated whether those advantages hold on over the long run or improve how long you live.

6.2 Atkins vs. other Diet Programs:

There are lots of diets available today to choose from, and during your search to lose weight, you might have attempted quite a few. Here's how Atkins relates to other popular weight loss plans, plus more examples of why Atkins should be selected.

Over 80 scientific trials confirm the productivity and health effects of low-carb diets like Atkins. Research has found that low-carb diets like Atkins contribute to more successful weight loss and improved healthcare outcomes by comparing weight loss programs, such as a decline in heart failure and diabetes risk. Plus, to help you reduce weight and hold it off, Atkins can be adjusted to your particular needs.

Some examples below clarify why you can prefer Atkins diet plan over other diet plans:

Weight Watchers vs. Atkins Diet:

How it works:

Based on your current weight, gender, height, and age, you are assigned a regular calorie budget.

Things one must eat:

All foods are approved with a given number of points for each item (which equates to calories). Based on your regular calorie budget, you can consume the number of points.

Why Atkins diet is better:

Calorie-counting diets might not be successful since all calories are not treated the same way by your body. Your body is prompted to store fat with refined carbohydrates, added sugar and empty carbohydrates. Calorie-counting diets do not show you the food's nutritional importance or why specific food decisions can be taken, i.e., eliminating items that can contribute to weight gain. In other terms, you might waste the whole day's budget of points on Fries or candy on Weight Watchers, which are not nutritionally wise options that encourage weight loss. It is no match, Atkins vs. Weight Watchers!

Mediterranean vs. Atkins Diet

How it works:

Eat just like the Mediterranean culture.

Food one must take:

Many plant-based diets (fruits and veggies), rice, whole-grain wheat, grains, seeds, and nuts are safe to consume. Tiny amounts of milk, cheese, meat and eggs, shellfish and fish, and fats (not butter), and you can consume herbs and spices twice a week. Cut back on desserts and red meat.

Why Atkins diet is better:

When you are carbohydrate insensitive, this diet is difficult since you might be eating more carbohydrates than your body can manage. You will learn to understand your tolerance for carbohydrates on Atkins, which will help you lose weight and sustain it. You are often required to eat higher protein levels, which helps keep you happy during meals for longer.

Paleo vs. Atkins Diet

How it works:

Eat the same meal that the hunter-gatherer descendants and pre-agricultural consumed.

Food one must eat:

Grass-fed meats, seafood/fish, new fruits and veggies, nuts/seeds, eggs, and organic oils could be consumed. Cereal crops, legumes (such as peanuts), dairy, added sugar, carbohydrates, canned meats, highly oily foods, and processed vegetable oils, processed candy/junk/and fast foods should be avoided.

Why Atkins diet is better:

It insists on the quality but not the number of carbs (meaning you might overdo it), and with its concentration on grass-fed meats and sustainable ingredients, Paleo is more strict than Atkins. You can use processed foods on Atkins, like low-carb bars, drinks, and meals, making it simpler to stick to the Atkins diet, and that you are allowed to consume legumes and milk.

Keto vs. Atkins diet:

How it works:

The purpose of the keto diet is to push your body to use a certain fuel type. The keto diet plan depends on the ketone bodies, a form of fuel that the liver generates from stored fat, instead of depending on sugar (glucose) from carbohydrates (like beans, legumes, fruits, and vegetables).

Food one must take:

Green beans, asparagus, shellfish, fish, cheese, cabbage, avocado, broccoli, cauliflower, cucumber, meat, green beans, eggplant, kale, lettuce, olives, eggs, olive oil.

Why Atkins diet is better?

For those searching for a less restrictive, quite familiar plan, Atkins might be a better match. Besides certain minor side effects such as fatigue, nausea, irritability and poor breath, little short-term health effects are being recorded for Atkins. Keto can pose health hazards for people with some medical problems and is not deemed safe for liver or kidney conditions. Dramatic effects on reproductive hormones and insulin can involve hormonal changes. The use of keto for diabetes patients remains problematic, especially for those taking insulin.

Why Atkins low carb diet wins:

Atkins is a simple winner when analyzing diets. You will customize the proportions and kinds of carbs you can consume while also being able to reduce weight or sustain a fat loss, and you will think about the regulation of portions and the consistency of your diet and how your weight loss is influenced. kPlus Atkins is endorsed by over 80 research trials and offers various healthy low-carb choices that help make things much simpler to adhere to the diet, such as shakes, snacks and frozen meals.

6.3 Recent research:

For quite a few years, this diet has been around, but its popularity has grown in the past decade. Over the last few years, the Atkins Diet has been a popular subject globally, and there are several web resources and community groups accessible where dieters can get guidance about different food concerns.

The diet would undoubtedly continue to be a divisive topic for years to come, given its huge celebrity following and regular press exposure. Every dieter who has any reservations over implementing such a strict dietary schedule should

As low-carb diets have risen in popularity, a variety of experiments have been performed by researchers to determine the efficacy and additional health consequences of the diets. The Harvard School of Public Health states that some evidence suggests that low-carb diets will help individuals shed weight faster and manage it more than low-fat diets would, and that moderately low-carb diets could be heart-healthy as long as healthier foods come from protein and fat choices.

A previous meta-analysis looked at 23 randomized trials of more than 2,500 participants. The researchers noticed that participants on a low-fat diet observed a slight yet statistically important reduction in overall cholesterol and triglyceride levels relative to participants on a low-fat diet, and at least comparable declines in weight, waist size, and other disease risk details. Another research, reported in The BMJ in October 2018, showed that low-carb dieters were able to sustain weight loss because, relative to those on a diet of higher carbohydrates, they burned around 200 extra calories per day.

A famous nutritionist Popeck cautions said: "Cutting out carbohydrates will initially lead to weight loss. However, it is possibly wasteful and deficient in nutrients to remove whole food classes, such as grains, milk, yogurt, and berries " "Fiber will definitely be lacking, as well as potassium, calcium and other vitamins and minerals." People interested in Atkins, but not consuming meat may opt to adopt the diet of Eco Atkins. The plan, established by researchers at Toronto's St. Michael's Hospital, has a comparable protein and carbohydrate ratio to the initial Atkins diet but substitutes vegetable protein with high-fat animal protein. For vegans and vegetarians, this diet is advisable. Customers that adopt a gluten-free lifestyle can have choices at Atkins. In addition to offering gluten-free meals, many gluten-free items are now sold by Atkins. Thus, the Atkins diet is the most well-known of the low-carb diets. The Atkins diet expects an extreme reduction in carbohydrates to less than 5 percent of the overall calorie consumption. The most contentious aspect of the Atkins plan is the simulated free-for-all consumption of as much protein and fat as you like.

Limiting sugary and starchy carbohydrates can help decrease calories and enable weight reduction for the individual who wants structure in their diet. And the safe and sensible thing to do is to rely on fats and proteins that are plant-based.

One must step away from the original Atkins 20 diet for your long-term wellbeing. It is the later stages of the diet that offer the range of foods that are necessary for health, particularly the Atkins 40. As you continue consuming almonds, peas, beans, vegetables and fruits, and whole grains again, and must work out and maintain portions small.

All of us try to cut out foods that we realize are terrible for us while trying to lose weight, be it fizzy beverages, indulgent sweets, or bread-based items. It is certain kinds of sugary, processed carbohydrates that will help you pack on weight. This makes common sense. You minimize the number of carbohydrates you consume with Atkins but take things much further: your body's metabolism switches to burning fat for energy. According to the firm, the items are not approved gluten-free by any third-party agency, but they fulfill the FDA's criteria.

The Atkins Plan, and others like it, went against the health recommendations and evidence that has been pushed out across the years: many nutritionists have been horrified by the prospect of a diet so high in fat and so poor in carbohydrates, and yet it has been shown to function. However, there are also questions among clinicians regarding the long-term effects that diets such as this can have.

Conclusion

While virtually thousands of fad diets are being marketed over the years, if we would not discuss the "Atkins Diet," the most popular mass diet of all times, we would be remiss. Robert Atkins created this high-protein, low-carbohydrate, high-fat diet. Dieters with allergies or hypersensitivity to grains, flour, and yeast could do quite well with this diet since carbohydrates are incredibly restricting and do not accommodate much in the way of bread or pasta, particularly during the initial crucial period.

However, eggs and fish, all of which are usually linked to food allergies, are key protein sources in this diet. Dieters should also make sure that they may not have an allergic reaction to foods like these before embarking on this plan. This would improve the diet's efficacy as well as decrease some health hazards. Try purchasing or lending one of the Atkins books if you are concerned about the Atkins diet, and please get started as soon as you can. Once of the followers of Atkins diet namely Shirley Hardy said:

"Atkins diet worked for me and there is no reason it cannot work for other people. I am 38 kg lighter now and the aching joints I suffered with when I was nearly 16 years old and it is a thing of the past. I have more energy and feel healthier than I have for a long time."

Ultimately, the safest diet for weight loss and other health issues is the one that a person practices to reach and sustain healthier body weight, so the Atkins diet is a strong and productive way to lose weight and stay healthy at the end of the day. You are not going to be disappointed.

Lightning Source UK Ltd.
Milton Keynes UK
UKHW031916250521
384380UK00006B/399

9 781802 039542